FINANCIAL MANAGEMENT AND INFLATION

FINANCIAL MANAGEMENT AND INFLATION

Harold Bierman, Jr.

with epigraphs by Florence M. Kelso

THE FREE PRESS
A Division of Macmillan Publishing Co., Inc.
NEW YORK

Collier Macmillan Publishers
LONDON

The Free Press
A Division of Macmillan Publishing Co., Inc.
866 Third Avenue, New York, N.Y. 10022

Collier Macmillan Canada, Ltd.

Library of Congress Catalog Card Number: 81-66987

Printed in the United States of America

printing number

1 2 3 4 5 6 7 8 9 10

Library of Congress Cataloging in Publication Data

Bierman, Harold.
  Financial management and inflation.

  Includes index.
  1. Corporations--Finance. 2. Accounting--Effect of
inflation on. 3. Industrial management--Effect of
inflation on. I. Title.
HG4026.B53   658.1'5   81-66987
ISBN 0-02-903570-8   AACR2

Contents

v

Preface

My forebearers, forged from sterner stuff,
Approved hard times. Things should be tough.
Perched on a gaunt, New England knee
I heard their grim philosophy:
If it hurt you
It was virtue;
If it be nice
Then it is vice.
This fundamental revelation
Implies there's merit in inflation.

FMK

Increasingly, inflation has become more and more a fact of life with which managers must learn to live. In this book we will consider analysis of accounting information and the making of financial decisions under conditions of inflation.

This book is the result of many conversations with executives where concerns with the impact of inflation on business affairs were expressed. Managers particularly wanted to find out how to bring inflation into the capital budgeting decision and how to measure performance under inflationary conditions.

Another question that has been raised is how to protect one's personal investments from the ravages of rapid inflation. While some sensible suggestions can be made (and are made in this book), one should not expect 100% panaceas that lead to a positive certain real return. Unfortunately, this author does not have a perfect forecasting device. We can define the risks and opportunities arising from inflationary conditions, but the best we can offer is a description of decision making under uncertainty. Sure cures for inflationary ills must be sought elsewhere. This author would be very surprised if you found such cures.

The study of inflation results in surprises. Some things we "know" about the effects of inflation on financial decision making turn out to have limited usefulness.

HAROLD BIERMAN, JR.

If the meaning is pithy
And the wording terse,
It is called an epigram
And not considered verse.

Constrained by subject matter,
Grim graphs, and computations
It's not likely I'll appear
In Bartlett's famed "Quotations."

But how about a second work?
If only there could be
A Bartlett's "Famous Epigrams"
—Including one by me!

FMK

FINANCIAL MANAGEMENT AND INFLATION

ONE

Inflation, Financial Analysis, and Accounting

When you must earn much more
To buy much less
The only winner is
The I.R.S.

FMK

Changes in the price level add interesting complexities to financial analysis. While the basic financial analysis techniques used in a noninflationary environment still apply, the interpretation of events is somewhat more difficult. Also, another level of complexity is added by inflation to the making of financial decisions.

A reader of this book is likely to conclude there are no easy answers for dealing with inflation. Given an uncertain world, "changing prices" only add one more element of uncertainty. In fact, without uncertainty there is no more problem coping with inflation than without inflation. Numbers change, but not the basic methods of analysis.

It is naive to conclude that everyone is harmed by inflation. Until calculations are made, we cannot be sure if inflation was helpful or harmful to a specific entity.

1

What Is Inflation?

We will define inflation to be an increase in the general price level. Inflation is easier to define than to measure because several difficulties exist. Not all prices increase proportionally; thus quantitative weights have to be determined for different products. The determination of weights is made more complex by change in consumption (usage) patterns. Also, product quality changes make it difficult to define what is a given product through time. The two more commonly used measures of the U.S. price level are the consumer price index and the GNP price deflators. Neither of these measures reflects perfectly the effect of changing prices on the well-being of a specific firm or a specific person, but they do give reasonably reliable measures of overall average price changes.

What Causes Inflation?

Introductory economics teaches us that inflation is caused by too much money chasing too few goods. In a sense we can say that inflation (the increase in prices) serves a very useful function because with the same amount of money and goods and without inflation there would be shortages or rationing.

In recent years two important contributing factors to inflationary pressures have been OPEC's control of an important factor of production and a tendency for productivity to increase marginally. An interest in improving the environment has also contributed, since pollution control and other possibly socially desirable achievements (such as safety) also impose explicit costs which tend to increase prices.

Structural rigidities in the economic system (strong unions and large corporations) combined with an effort by the federal government and the Federal Reserve to achieve full employment by injecting money into the system have tended to fuel the inflation.

Finally, once inflationary expectations become widespread, they lead to decisions which in turn are inflationary. For example, wages indexed to a price level measure will tend to contribute to the next round of price increases.

What Has Been the Inflation?

When one complains about inflation, one is complaining about the fact that the prices of the things being bought are now more expensive than they were in past time periods. Table 1-1 shows the implicit price deflators of the U.S. gross national product from 1967 to 1979. Prices have more than doubled since 1967.

Table 1-2 shows the consumer price index (CPI) for the same period. The existence of price inflation is again made obvious.

A person living in an economic environment where prices are increasing at a rate of 100% per year (e.g., Argentina and Brazil) is

TABLE 1-1. Implicit Price Deflators for Gross National Product*

YEAR	INDEX
1967	79.0
1968	82.6
1969	86.7
1970	91.4
1971	96.0
1972	100.0
1973	105.8
1974	116.0
1975	127.2
1976	133.9
1977	141.7
1978	152.1
1979	165.5

* *Business Statistics,* 1977 edition, U.S. Department of Commerce, and *Survey of Current Business,* January 1980.

TABLE 1-2.   The Consumer Price Index*

YEAR	INDEX
1967	100.0
1968	104.2
1969	109.8
1970	116.3
1971	121.3
1972	125.3
1973	133.1
1974	147.7
1975	161.2
1976	170.5
1977	181.5
1978	195.3
1979	229.0

* *Handbook of Labor Statistics, 1978,* U.S. Department of Labor, and *Survey of Current Business,* January 1980.

going to smile at a United States consumer complaining at the rate of inflation in the United States. But a person in the United States who saw $100,000 of bonds reduced in purchasing power to less than $50,000 from 1967 to 1979 is not going to find the situation humorous.

Inflation of any magnitude harms a wide range of persons. It is small comfort for a specific person so harmed to be told it is worse in some other part of the globe.

A 10% inflation rate per year means that prices double every seven years (approximately). This is significant even if a 20% inflation rate may be twice as bad.

Measuring the results of business activities is difficult with constant prices. An element of additional complexity is introduced with rapidly changing prices.

We first want to consider the use of conventional accounting with inflation. Our conclusion will be that historical cost based accounting supplies useful information for managers and investors but other useful information is omitted; thus adjustment may be needed for selected purposes.

Income

Consider the simplest situation, where there are revenues but no expenses (an alternative condition would be where there are no ending real assets). A firm earns $1,000 of cash in year 1 and $1,100 of cash in year 2. Conventional accounting measures indicate that income has increased, and a naive conclusion follows that the firm is better off in period 2 than in period 1.

Now add the information that the price index went from 100 in year 1 to 120 in year 2. Deflating the income of year 2 for the inflation gives $1,100/1.20 = $917 in terms of beginning of the year purchasing power, and we see that the price level adjusted income (the real income) has actually decreased in year 2 compared to that of year 1. The monetary income of year 2 ($1,100) is larger, but the real income ($917) is lower in year 2 than in year 1.

The firm did actually earn $1,000 of cash in period 1 and $1,100 in period 2, and these are useful measures. For example, if the debt payments are to be $1,050 in period 2, we know the firm will have sufficient income to pay its debt. The conventional income measures become deficient when an attempt is made to compare the incomes of successive periods and to use the unadjusted income measures to conclude the relative degree of well-being in the different periods. We cannot conclude that $1,100 in period 2 is an improvement over $1,000 in period 1, given that there was .20 inflation.

Normally there are two problems. One is the measurement of the period's income and the second is the comparison of the incomes of successive years. Above there was no problem in measuring the income of a period, and we focused on the problem of comparing the purchasing power of incomes of successive years.

Choice of the Price Index

Price indexes are averages. They reflect the change in the ability to purchase a given market basket of goods. If you are not going to purchase that exact market basket, then the index does not measure exactly the effect of the changing prices on your well-being.

Consider the above example. All corporations artificially lumped together are assumed to have one average market basket of goods. But even corporations in the same industry would have a different set of goods. The specific firm being studied will buy a different collection of goods (in different localities) than other firms in the same industry. An index based on this latter set of goods would be more useful in judging the well-offness of a specific firm being analyzed. But computing a different index for each firm would be expensive, and its application would make comparison of the operating results of several firms terribly complex.

But the choice of indexes does not end with those described above. Rather than consider the goods that the firm (or other corporations) will buy, we can shift our attention to the goods that the owners of the firm will buy to answer the question whether their financial situation has improved through time. There is then the choice of the consumer price index, the wholesale-price index, or the price adjustors used to deflate the gross national product to adjust for inflation.

We will find it convenient in this book to speak of the use of a price index without clearly specifying the exact nature of the index. For certain purposes the purchasing power of the corporation is relevant, and for other purposes we are interested in the well-being of the investors. The purpose of the calculation will influence which index should be used.

Measuring Income: The Inventory Problem

As soon as we move from the simplest situation described above where there were no expenses and income was easily defined to one where expenses exist, the analysis of an income stream can become more complex. We will assume assets are acquired, placed in inventory, and then sold. An inventory cost flow problem exists. For simplication we assume there are no fixed assets.

Conventional accounting offers many cost flow assumptions, but we will only consider first-in, first-out (FIFO), and last-in, first-out (LIFO), and replacement cost measures.

Assume the firm starts with the following balance sheet:

Cash	$ 500
Inventory (two units)	1,500
Stockholders' equity	$2,000

Now assume one unit is sold for $900 and another unit of identical inventory is purchased for cash at a cost of $950. There are no other expenses than cost of goods sold. All units in inventory, sold, and purchased are homogeneous.

What do we know? We know that the cash at the end of the period is $450, a decrease of $50, and that the firm has two units in inventory, the last unit costing $950. That is all we know. Other conclusions will be based on assumptions.

We can compare the beginning and ending positions. The firm started with $500 of cash and two units in inventory. The firm ended with $450 of cash and the same physical inventory. This analysis indicates the firm was worse off by $50. Using the LIFO method of accounting, we have a $50 loss:

Revenues	$ 900
Cost of goods sold	950
Loss	$ 50

The ending balance sheet is:

Cash	$ 450
Inventory	1,500
Stockholders' equity	$1,950

The $50 loss and the $50 decrease in stock equity agree with the verbal analysis that concluded that the firm is worse off by $50.

But let us consider a different method of evaluation. At the beginning of the period the firm had command over $2,000 of resources. At the end of the period the firm had $450 of cash and two units of inventory which on a replacement cost basis are worth $1,900. The total ending resources are $2,350. This is $350 more than at the beginning of the period. Using FIFO we obtain:

Revenue	$ 900
Cost of goods sold	750
Income	$ 150

The balance sheet is:

Cash	$ 450
Inventory	1,700
Stockholders' equity	$2,150

FIFO indicates an improvement of $150, but the verbal analysis concluded the improvement was $350. The reconciling factor is the $200 unrealized (and unrecognized) appreciation in the value of the one unit in inventory not sold which cost $750 and which has a replacement cost of $950 at the end of the period.

The LIFO measure of income (a loss of $50) is useful if we want to ignore the change in value (as well as ignoring the cost) of the inventory that is held.

FIFO gives a measure of income if we want to include the change in the value of the inventory as income. If all the beginning inventory is sold, the measure will reflect the total change in value. If some of the beginning inventory is not sold, the FIFO method will not includle the market value change on these units of inventory (the $200 of unrealized gain in the above example).

Was there a loss of $50 or a gain of $150 or $350, or something else? Both the LIFO and FIFO measures of income have significance. It is important to interpret properly the income measure and the balance sheet that results.

If a firm is purchasing inventory at a cost of $950, it would be uneconomic to sell a unit at $900 and then immediately replace the unit at a cost of $950. Two sensible decisions are possible. One is to liquidate, that is, sell the units at $900 and not replace. The second is to hold the two units until the selling price reflects the $950 replacement cost. The proper decision does not depend on the results of the accounting method. We could prepare the income statement using the $950 replacement cost, but the $50 loss resulting from selling one unit for $900 is not the complete story. One would also have to report the $200 realized market gain ($950 − $750) and $200 of unrealized gain.

A reasonably complete description is to say that there was a $50 operating loss and $400 of market gain from holding inventory or a $350 net gain (realized and unrealized). There is a $350 increase in command over resources.

But even this $350 of net gain cannot be compared to the income of the previous year, since the dollars have not been adjusted for changes in purchasing power (the $1,000 of income for period 1 and $1,100 of income for period 2 of the first example could not be compared without first adjusting for purchasing power changes).

In the situation where one unit is sold for $900 and replaced for $950, we can compare the command over resources at the beginning of the period ($500 + $1,500) with the command over resources at the end ($450 + $1,900 = $2,350). The $350 increase can be called income and is equal to the income that results from the use of replacement cost for all the inventory and cost of goods sold.

The Choice for Taxes

The economic choice for tax calculation purposes is simple. For tax planning purposes LIFO dominates FIFO as long as prices are increasing. Assume that the LIFO cost of goods sold is $10,-000,000 larger than the FIFO cost. With a .46 tax rate the choice of LIFO results in the savings of $4,600,000. The choice of LIFO is worth $4,600,000 now to the firm, and more savings will occur each year.

It is true that the accounting measure of income will be reduced by $5,400,000 with the shift to LIFO, but the financial market is not naive. Note is taken by investors of the method that is used to account for inventory.

Long-lived Assets

The economic analysis of long-lived assets is analogous to that of inventory, with the added complexity that the asset is expensed over a large number of years.

We want first to illustrate a situation where the conventional accounting, without adjustment, does a very useful job.

Assume that an investment costs $3,000 and will have the following cash flows. These cash flows reflect the assumption that a .10 annual inflation takes place:

Time	Cash Flow
0	− 3,000
1	1,600
2	1,400
3	1,200

The firm uses a straight line method of depreciation and a .20 discount rate to evaluate investments.

If the .10 annual inflation takes place and if the cash flows are exactly as forecast, the results from operations will be:

PERIOD	CASH FLOW	DEPRECIATION	INCOME	BEGINNING INVESTMENT	RETURN ON INVESTMENT
1	1,600	1,000	600	3,000	.20
2	1,400	1,000	400	2,000	.20
3	1,200	1,000	200	1,000	.20

These reporting results are very satisfactory. In fact, any price level adjustment is likely to introduce a distortion. The .20 internal rate of return that was forecast when the investment was undertaken actually occurs, with the result that the return on investment of each year is equal to .20.

Admittedly, this was a very special situation. The actual inflation was perfectly anticipated at the time of investment, and the forecast cash flows were related to each other in a very special fashion.

Most importantly the example illustrates dramatically the fact that if the inflation is not a surprise, but rather is anticipated, adjustments to depreciation and long-lived assets for price level changes may not be necessary.

There are four basic measures which are of interest:

1. Depreciated cost
2. Depreciated cost adjusted by a price index adjusting for inflation.
3. Replacement cost
4. Present value of the remaining cash flows associated with the asset

With constant prices all four measures can be equal, but this is unlikely even with constant prices.

If there had been inflation, depreciated cost and depreciated cost adjusted by a price index cannot equal each other, but it is theoretically possible for three of the measures to be equal.

However, it is more likely for all the four measures to be different. Which measure is relevant? The present value of the remaining cash flows associated with the asset is the only one of the four measures relevant for decision-making purposes, from a theoretical point of view. But the present value measure has two major drawbacks. It is highly subjective and thus difficult to verify, and in addition there is not general agreement as to the method of calculation, even if there were agreement as to the values of the inputs.

As long as the accounting profession avoids present value measures because of their highly subjective nature and chooses instead more easily measured and less relevant measures, there will be major difficulties using the accounting information as the basis for making decisions. This conclusion follows whether or not there is inflation, and whether or not the cost based information is adjusted for price level changes.

With inflation the more long-lived assets a firm possesses, the less reliable the accounting measures become as estimators of value.

In fact, one of the few asset values measured in less reliable fashion than long-lived real assets and depreciable assets is the value of intangible assets resulting from research and development expenditures. These expenditures are expensed, thus insuring a zero value on the financial statements for the knowledge derived as a result of the expenditures. The one virtue of this practice is that it is well known that the published statements understate this asset (as well as other intangible assets).

A Likely Winner

The federal government is a likely winner when there is rapid inflation. Inflation has the effect of decreasing the real value of the presently outstanding debt, thus improving the financial position of the government. It will also increase the monetary value of the real assets owned by the government. But most importantly, with progressive income tax rates, inflation tends to move taxpayers into higher tax brackets. The average tax rate for a given amount of consumer purchasing power is increased.

An additional benefit to government is that the real value of business tax deductions is reduced, thus increasing the real effective tax rate that corporations pay. Inflation is particularly harsh on long-lived assets, since the value of their tax shields (depreciation expense) is greatly eroded by inflation rates of any significant magnitude.

Conclusions

If a firm buys an asset for $750 and sells it for $900, it has made $150 of income; however, there may be other gains and losses. This analysis and conclusion is the basis of conventional cost based accounting. It applies to a firm holding both inventory and long-lived assets.

It is well to keep the above example in mind. It is simple and informative. Naive cost based accounting supplies useful measures of income.

But the above example is excessively simplified, and as we make the example more realistic, we will find that other price level adjusted measures of income and financial position are also of interest. Costs expressed in current purchasing power may be more relevant for decisions than the costs which are a historical accident. Even though a firm sells an asset costing $750 for $900, it might be economically worse off at the end of the period than at the beginning. A method of accounting that reveals this situation is described in the next chapter.

The point of departure for financial analysis is the fact that if a firm buys a product for $750 and sells it for $900, it has made a profit if there are no additional complexities. The profit may not be as much as it would like, and it may not be as much as the firm made last period. If the firm then buys another unit for $950, it is starting a new cycle of operations, and presumably buying the unit because it expects to sell the new unit for more than $950. If this expectation does not exist, it is difficult to explain the logic that led to the purchase of the unit costing $950.

Key Ideas to Remember

1. Complexity is introduced by inflation only when inflation is combined with uncertainty.

2. Not everyone is harmed by inflation. The federal government is a likely winner.

3. With inflation there are problems in measuring income and also problems in comparing incomes of successive years.

4. Since price indexes are averages, they are unlikely to measure changes in prices or costs of a specific firm or person.

5. Inflation is a substitute for shortages or rationing with a given supply of money and goods.

6. With inflation the use of LIFO results in significant immediate tax savings and additional savings through time.

TWO

Constant Dollar Accounting: A Primer

As a nation
Our relation
With inflation
Is a bummer—
No sensation
Of elation
No vacation
Come next summer.
                    FMK

In Chapter 1 we briefly considered how changes in the price level affect the measurement of real assets, inventory, and plant assets of a firm. We will now expand the discussion to consider the constant dollar accounting procedure.

Assume a situation where a firm has one asset, cash, at the beginning and end of the period. The cash balance (financed entirely by common stock) increased from $1,000 to $1,500. There was a $500 operating gain, and the stockholders' equity also increased from $1,000 to $1,500. Let us now add the information that the general price index was 100 at the beginning of the period and 150 at the end. The firm (and its owners) had $1,000 of purchasing power at both the beginning and the end of the period in terms of beginning of the year dollars, and we would say that there was no "real" income, but merely a change in the dollar

15

description of the financial positions at two points in time. An accounting measure of $500 of income may be misleading. This section analyzes how changes in the general purchasing power of the dollar may be incorporated into the accounting measures. FAS 33 of the Financial Accounting Standards Board comes close to being consistent with the constant dollar accounting described in this chapter, but there are differences. For example, FAS 33 uses average price indexes, and we will use the end of the period.

Constant dollar accounting is a method of systematically recognizing the effect of changes in the general price level in the accounting records. The objective of the procedure is to measure as income real increments in the well-being of the corporate entity and to subtract out from the measurement of income all changes in dollar valuation that do not reflect an improvement in financial position. For example, assume the following balance sheet:

January 1

Inventory (100 units at $2)	$200
Stockholders' equity	$200

Assume there are no transactions during January, but that there is a doubling of all prices and this change is reflected in a doubling of a general price index series. If the ending inventory is expressed in terms of the year end value, the balance sheet at the end of accounting period would be:

January 31

Inventory (100 units at $4)	$400
Stockholders' equity	$400

Note that the inventory is stated in terms of present market prices and it would seem that there has been a market gain of $200. Constant dollar accounting would restate the January 1 statement in period end dollars, and the two balance sheets would be:

	January 1	January 31
Inventory (restated in terms of period end dollars)	$400	$400
Stockholders' equity (restated in terms of period end dollars)	$400	$400

Because the beginning and ending balance sheets are identical, the conclusion is that there was not a gain or loss during the period. We started the period with 100 units of product and ended with 100 units. The dollar expression of the 100 units at the end of the period was different than at the beginning, but if we express both the beginning and ending information in terms of the same types of dollars, we find the market gain disappears. This differs from the section of the previous chapter that discussed inventories. The reconciling factor is that in the prior section we were discussing income in terms of dollars and ignoring the purchasing power of the dollars. In this section, we are dealing with income in real terms and are not interested in market gains which merely result from a change in the method of describing a physical unit in terms of dollars. A real asset financed with common stock does not result in a market gain if constant dollar accounting is used.

The same analysis carries over to the accounting for fixed assets using the constant dollar method. There are no gains from holding fixed assets during inflation. If we buy a house for $20,000 cash and the price level doubles and the house is now worth $40,000, constant dollar accounting would say that we did not have a real gain. Restating the value of the house and our equity in the house in terms of end of the period dollars would indicate that we had $40,000 of house at the beginning and end of the period; thus we did not have a gain. It is possible that if we did not buy the house and retained cash, we would be worse off than we are now, but the conclusion still remains that we did not actually benefit from buying the house. A real gain does result from holding real assets financed wholly or partially with debt, but the mechanics of the constant dollar accounting procedure associate that gain with the monetary items.

Thus, in constant dollar accounting, gains and losses are not directly associated with holding fixed assets or inventories. If a real asset changes in dollar value as the price level changes, constant dollar accounting will not indicate gains or losses resulting from these price level changes. The gains or losses arise from holding assets whose dollar value remains constant as the price level changes, or from being in debt and having the amount that we have to pay remain a fixed sum in terms of dollars. We term items of this nature monetary accounts. Monetary accounts include cash, accounts receivable, other fixed dollar claims, and liabilities.

Assume a firm has the following balance sheet:

January 1

Cash	$300
Stockholders' equity	$300

The price level at January 1 is 100, and at January 31 it is 200. Assume no financial transactions took place during January. Following both conventional accounting and constant dollar accounting, the balance sheet at January 31 would be the same as indicated above. While the comparative balance sheets of the two time periods would be identical for conventional accounting, they would differ considerably for constant dollar accounting.

CONSTANT DOLLAR ACCOUNTING
USING YEAR END PURCHASING POWER

	January 1	*January 31*
Cash	$600	$300
Stockholders' equity	$600	$300

For constant dollar accounting there would be need for an income statement showing a monetary loss of $300 (in terms of period end dollars) arising from holding cash during a period of inflation. The loss is computed as follows:

Opening balance in terms of period end dollars:

$$\$300 \times \frac{200}{300} = \$600$$

Expected ending balance in terms of period end dollars	$600
Less actual ending balance per accounting records	300
Monetary loss from holding cash	$300

The $300 balance at the beginning of the month is equivalent to $600 of purchasing power expressed in terms of period end dollars. At the end of the month we only have $300 of cash in terms of month end dollars; because there were no explicit transactions, there must have been a monetary loss of $300.

While the firm will incur a loss if it holds cash during a period of inflation, it will benefit from being in debt. Assume the balance sheets as of January 1 and January 31 are as follows:

	January 1	*January 31*
Cash	$300	$300
Current liabilities	200	200
Stockholders' equity	100	100

If the price level doubles from January 1 to January 31, the constant dollar balance sheets for the two time periods will be as follows:

CONSTANT DOLLAR ACCOUNTING

	January 1	*January* 31
Cash	$600	$300
Current liabilities	400	200
Stockholders' equity	200	100
	$600	$300

We have already computed the monetary loss of $300 from holding cash during the month of inflation. The monetary gain of being in debt is as follows:

Expected ending balance in terms of period end dollars	$400
Less actual balance per accounting records	200
Monetary gain from being in debt	$200

The liability at the beginning of the period was $400 (in terms of period end dollars), but the liability at the end of period was only $200; thus there was a $200 gain arising from being in debt during the inflation period.

The total monetary gains and losses were a $300 loss from holding cash and a $200 gain from being in debt; the net loss from all monetary items was $100. This is equal to the decrease in the stockholders' equity.

Long-Term Debt

Assume a $100,000 plant is financed completely with debt and there is a doubling of the price level. The balance sheets assuming constant dollar accounting are:

	Beginning	*End*
Plant	$200,000	$200,000
Debt	200,000	100,000
Stockholders' equity	$ 0	$100,000

The above statements use end of period purchasing power measures.

Stockholders' equity changes from zero to $100,000. This reflects the $100,000 monetary gain from being in debt.

The monetary gains and losses on monetary current assets and current liabilities are generally assumed to be realized as the price level changes. In the case of long-term debt outstanding, there is some disagreement among accountants as to whether this gain is ever realized if the corporation normally has the same amount of debt outstanding. In a period of inflation, instead of recognizing the gain arising from having long-term debt outstanding, these accountants suggest that the monetary gain would not affect the income of the period.

Recognizing the difficulty of determining criteria for the realization of gains of this nature, there is nevertheless sufficient justification for considering the gains on long-term debt to be analogous to gains on short-term debt. The moment of realization depends not only on the nature of the debt but also on the nature of the assets in which the funds generated by this debt have been used. For example, assume that $100,000 worth of bonds have been issued to finance the purchase of a building. The price level immediately doubles and the building is sold, but the bonds are not retired. In this case, the balance sheet at the beginning of the period is:

Building	100,000	Bonds	100,000
		Stockholders' equity	0
	100,000		100,000

After the sale of the building the balance sheet is:

Cash	200,000	Bonds	100,000
		Stockholders' equity	100,000
	200,000		200,000

The stockholders have made a gain of $100,000 expressed in end of the period dollars, and the gain is further evidenced by the fact that $200,000 of cash is available to pay off $100,000 of debt. The realization of the gain in this simple case is not contingent on the retirement of the bonds. If the example is made more complicated and the building is not sold outright but rather is depreciated, this tends to hide the nature of the transactions which are occurring. But long-term debt does give rise to monetary gains and losses that may be treated in the same manner as those associated with current monetary assets and liabilities. Both current and long-term monetary gains and losses are relevant in measuring income.

A More Complex Example

COMPARATIVE BALANCE SHEETS
(CONVENTIONAL ACCOUNTING)

	January 1	December 31
Cash	$ 20,000	$ 50,000
Building	100,000	100,000
Less accumulated depreciation	(40,000)	(50,000)
	$ 80,000	$100,000
Current liabilities	$ 10,000	$ 10,000
Bonds payable	50,000	50,000
Stockholders' equity	20,000	40,000
	$ 80,000	$100,000

Transactions for the year included the following:

1. Sales of $100,000 all for cash
2. Out-of-pocket expenses of $70,000
3. Annual depreciation expense of $10,000

An index of the general price level indicated the following:

Date	Price Index
January 1	100
December 31	200

The building was purchased when the price level was 50.

All transactions are assumed to have occurred evenly throughout the year at an average price level of 150.

Required: Prepare comparative balance sheets and income statements with all items expressed in dollars of year end purchasing power.

Solution to Example

CASH

$20,000 × $\frac{200}{100}$ = 40,000　　Year end dollars
　　　　　　　　　　　　　　　　(opening balance)

$30,000 × $\frac{200}{150}$ = 40,000　　Year end dollars
　　　　　　　　　　　　　　　　(net cash receipts)

Expected balance　　80,000

Balance per books　　50,000

Monetary loss　　　　30,000

ACCOUNTS PAYABLE

Expected balance 10,000 × $\frac{200}{100}$ = 20,000

Balance per books　　　　　　　　　10,000

Monetary gain　　　　　　　　　　　10,000

BONDS PAYABLE

Expected balance 50,000 × $\frac{200}{100}$ = 100,000

Balance per books　　　　　　　　　50,000

Monetary gain　　　　　　　　　　　50,000

INCOME STATEMENTS FOR YEAR ENDING DECEMBER 31
(ALL ITEMS IN YEAR END DOLLARS)

	Conventional	*Constant Dollar*
Sales	100,000 × $\frac{200}{150}$ =	133,333
Less:		
Expenses	70,000 × $\frac{200}{150}$ =	93,333
Depreciation	10,000 × $\frac{200}{50}$ =	40,000
	80,000	133,333
Operating income	20,000	0
Monetary gain (60,000 less 30,000)		30,000
Net Income		30,000

COMPARATIVE BALANCE SHEETS
(All Items in Year End Dollars)

	January 1	December 31
Cash	40,000	50,000
Building	400,000	400,000
Less accumulated depreciation	(160,000)	(200,000)
	280,000	250,000
Accounts payable	20,000	10,000
Bonds payable	100,000	50,000
Stockholders' equity	160,000	190,000
	280,000	250,000

The above statements adjust the long-lived assets using the historical cost information as the basis of the adjustment.

For reasons to be described in a later chapter the price level adjusted information presented in the comparative balance sheets may not be reliable measures of value (especially where the price level changes were anticipated by the decision makers).

Note that the change in the stockholders' equity indicated in the balance sheet is equal to that amount shown on the bottom of the income statement.

Constant Dollar Accounting and Management

While FAS 33 is a step toward constant dollar accounting, constant dollar accounting is not universally accepted for general financial accounting and reporting purposes. It is thought that the use of index numbers to make the adjustment is not objective and the end results are too difficult to analyze. For example, the total sales figure would not be the total dollars of sales accrued, but rather the total sales converted into constant dollar measures. FAS 33 does not adjust revenues or costs incurred in the period being reviewed since an average price index is used. There is also the problem of the choice of the price index series that should be used to make the adjustments. Even if there were agreement that it should be a general price index, the exact construction of the index would be subject to argument.

Is constant dollar accounting of use for internal managerial purposes? Assume a corporation has a division operating in a foreign country we shall call Utopia. Utopia has had a continuing inflation of the magnitude of a 50 per cent increase in price level per year. Conventional accounting procedures may not give an effective measure of the efficiency of the division in Utopia. Inflation can hide inefficiencies, and conventional accounting ignores the market gains and losses associated with the monetary assets. Thus, to measure the real change in value one might turn to reports prepared in terms of constant dollar accounting. It is true that the reports would require interpretation, but once understood they would be usefully complementary to the conventional accounting reports (remember Utopia has a high degree of inflation). Constant dollar accounting reports an income figure that incorporates all changes in asset position, including the changes in real value in monetary assets and liabilities. In terms of judging the performance of someone who has complete control of an operation, this would seem to be a desirable reporting objective.

Instead of reporting on the division in Utopia (with an increase in price level of 50 per cent per year), let us assume the division is located in the country of Exurbia where the inflation is approximately 2 per cent per year. Here again, constant dollar accounting could be used and would present useful information. But is the value of the information worth the added confusion associated with the method? There is no question that interpretation of the constant dollar accounting reports requires a higher level of accounting sophistication than conventional accounting. Where the rate of inflation is relatively small it is an open question whether the information value of the constant dollar accounting reports is more than conventional accounting reports. If the rate of inflation is large, than a good argument can be made for the use of supplemental reports using constant dollar accounting.

Constant dollar accounting is particularly useful in comparing how well off a firm is at the end of a period compared to the beginning of the period, though significant problems of price level adjustments for long-lived assets remain.

Selected Bibliography

ALEXANDER, S. S., "Income Measurement in a Dynamic Economy," reprinted in W. T. Baxter and S. Davidson, *Studies in Accounting Theory* (Homewood, Ill.: R.D. Irwin, 1962).

EDWARDS, E. O., and BELL, P. W., *The Theory and Measurement of Business Income* (Berkeley: University of California Press, 1961).

Key Ideas to Remember

1. With constant dollar accounting there is not a real gain if real assets are financed with stock equity capital.

2. With constant dollar accounting there is a real gain if real assets are financed with debt.

3. FAS 33 is a step toward constant dollar accounting but differs in substantive ways.

4. Constant dollar accounting is useful in measuring how well off an entity is at successive moments in time.

5. While there are monetary gains from financing real assets with debt during inflation, we cannot conclude that using debt is desirable.

6. The realization of a monetary gain with long-term debt does not require the retirement of the debt.

7. Conventional accounting does not tell the user of the reports whether the entity is economically better off at the end of the period than at the beginning.

THREE

Accounting Practice: FAS No. 33

> *Inflation*
> *Will ration*
> *The goods of*
> *The nation.*
>   *FMK*

The Statement of Financial Accounting Standards No. 33, "Financial Reporting and Changing Prices," is an experiment by the FASB that requires that major U.S. companies disclose the effects of changing prices as supplementary information in their published annual reports. Since top managers of corporations generally want to know how a decision will affect the financial statements of a firm, we can expect that pro forma financial statements will be prepared for proposed investments. Unfortunately there will be some real decision distortions introduced by the type of price level accounting recommended by FAS 33. It is likely that desirable investments will be deemed to be undesirable when the price level accounting effects are taken into consideration. The difficulty arises because the price level accounting recommended by FAS 33 has very specific objectives, and when the technique is used generally, many problems are introduced.

J. E. Connor, the chairman of Price Waterhouse & Co., has written:[1]

> The FASB should explain, and preferably illustrate, precisely how the results of applying current measurement concepts will be more useful than historical concepts for making economic decisions, for predicting future cash flows, for evaluating investment alternatives, and so on.

Mr. Connor is correct, since it is naive to assume that the method of accounting will not affect economic decisions. Unfortunately, "second best" accounting procedures will frequently lead to inferior decision processes.

FAS 33 requires large companies to experiment with two methods of reporting under inflationary conditions. With one method the adjustments are made using the measures of the general price level (the procedure is called constant dollar accounting). The second method is called current cost accounting, and it uses specific price changes.

FAS 33 suggests a simplified version of constant dollar accounting. Costs which originated in prior periods (inventory cost of goods sold and depreciation expense) are adjusted using a general price index. The income measure on which earnings per share are based is computed without including the monetary gains and losses. The monetary gains and losses are computed and shown separately, but do not affect the earnings per share figure shown.

FAS 33 requires three earnings per share measures; one is based on historical cost information, and the other two are the "Income (loss) from continuing operations per common share" using constant dollar or current cost information. These latter two measures exclude the holding gains and losses ("Gain from decline in purchasing power of net amounts owed"). This exclusion means that the price level adjusted earnings per share measures presented are incomplete measures with potential for in-

---

[1]J. E. Connor, *Accounting for the Effects of Inflation: It's About Time!* published by Price Waterhouse & Co., New York, 1979.

troducing distortion into the decision processes of corporations, as well as the evaluation of financial affairs. While we focus on Schedule C, it should be realized that even a theoretically correct price level accounting procedure could not be used to evaluate in-

EXHIBIT 1.   Extract from Weyerhaeuser Company's 1979 Annual Report

Following is the supplementary financial information required by Statement No. 33:

Consolidated Earnings Adjusted for Changing Prices

		ADJUSTED FOR	
FOR THE YEAR ENDED DECEMBER 30, 1979	AS REPORTED	GENERAL INFLATION	SPECIFIC PRICES
Net sales	$4,422,653	$4,422,653	$4,422,653
Weyerhaeuser Real Estate Company earnings	57,117	57,117	57,117
Other income, net	37,005	37,005	37,005
	4,516,775	4,516,775	4,516,775
Operating costs and expenses:			
Other than depreciation, amortization and fee stumpage—Note A	3,340,630	3,350,171	3,349,721
Depreciation, amortization and fee stumpage	332,594	501,157	509,920
Interest expense	104,607	104,607	104,607
	3,777,831	3,955,935	3,964,248
Earnings before income taxes	738,944	560,840	552,527
Income taxes	226,700	226,700	226,700
Net earnings	$ 512,244	$ 334,140	$ 325,827
Per common share	$ 4.02	$ 2.59	$ 2.52
Gain from decline in the purchasing power of net amounts owed		$ 174,012	$ 174,012

Note A: The Company used the last-in, first-out (LIFO) method of accounting for product inventories. Operating costs have been adjusted to give effect to changing prices upon liquidations of LIFO layers during the current year.

(*continued*)

EXHIBIT 1. (*Cont.*)

Net Assets for Changing Prices

	As Reported	ADJUSTED FOR	
DECEMBER 30, 1979		GENERAL INFLATION	SPECIFIC PRICES
Product inventories	$ 341,301	$ 457,974	$ 515,203
Materials and supplies	124,141	131,726	132,524
Property and equipment	2,485,243	3,373,996	3,457,257
Timber and timberlands	608,312	1,463,519	1,463,519
Leased property under capital leases	150,608	180,399	180,399
All other assets, net	396,023	396,023	396,023
	4,105,628	6,003,637	6,144,925
Deduct net monetary liabilities	1,369,761	1,369,761	1,369,761
Net assets	$2,735,867	$4,633,876	$4,775,164

vestments without careful analysis. FAS 33 unnecessarily widens the gap between accounting and investment decision making. Exhibit 1 is an extract from Weyerhaeuser Company's 1979 annual report. It shows the application of FAS 33's Schedule C. Note that the gain from the decline in purchasing power is inserted after the calculation of the earnings per share. The adjustment in depreciation expense affects the earnings per share, but the monetary gain from being in debt does not. This is consistent with the dictates of FAS 33. The $2.59 earnings per share calculation is the constant dollar accounting income measure.

We shall use a simplified example to illustrate the problems introduced into decision making by FAS 33. The only crucial assumption made is that the top level decision makers consider the impact of a decision on the pro forma accounting information resulting from the decision. This assumption would seem to be reasonable.

An Example: No Inflation

Let us consider the following investment in a situation where there is no price level accounting. The firm requires a .18 return for an investment to be acceptable. To avoid unnecessary complexity, we assume a zero tax rate.

TIME	CASH FLOW
0	− 3,000
1	1,600
2	1,400
3	1,200

The investment has a .20 discounted cash flow internal rate of return, and using the .18 as a rate of discount, we obtain a $92 net present value. The investment seems to be acceptable, but assume that the management wants to know the effect on income and the accounting return on investment (using conventional accounting and the beginning of the period investment). Using straight line depreciation to compute income, we obtain:

PERIOD	CASH FLOW	DEPRECIATION	INCOME	BEGINNING INVESTMENT	ROI
1	1,600	1,000	600	3,000	.20
2	1,400	1,000	400	2,000	.20
3	1,200	1,000	200	1,000	.20

The ROI of each period is .20, and the average ROI is equal to the discounted cash flow rate of return. The investment is clearly acceptable.

The conclusion that the investment is acceptable is independent of information about the general or specific price levels. While actually only the net present value of the cash flows needs to be computed, a calculation of income and ROI is entirely consistent with the accept decision.

We could change the example and have a situation where the economic analyis indicated that the investment was acceptable but the accounting information moved management to reject. But this new problem can be solved by modifying the method of depreciation from the straight line method to a more theoretically correct method of calculation. In the example being studied the straight line method is both relatively simple to compute and reasonably theoretically correct.

The Price Level Adjustment

We will now illustrate the consequences on the investment decision of price level accounting consistent with FAS 33. Assume the same facts as above except we will now reveal that there is a .10 inflation per year expected for the next three years (both the general and specific prices are expected to increase the same amount). The projected cash flows are based on this expected inflation rate. Assume the investment has certain cash flows and will be financed with debt costing .18. The investment is clearly desirable.

We will assume that management is interested in the pro forma accounting resulting from the proposed investment and will focus on the income from continuing operations and the ROI obtained from using that income measure. The depreciation expense is now adjusted for the inflation, but the cost of the investment is used as the base for the adjustment:

Period	Cash Flow	Price Level Adjusted Depreciation	Price Level Adjusted Income from Continuing Operations	ROI
1	1,600	1,000 × 1.10 = 1,100	500	.167
2	1,400	1,000 × 1.21 = 1,210	190	.095
3	1,200	1,000 × 1.331 = 1,331	− 131	negative

The average ROI for the three years is:

$$\text{Average ROI} = \frac{(500 + 190 - 131)\frac{1}{3}}{1,500} = \frac{(559)\frac{1}{3}}{1,500} = .12$$

The required return of .18 is not earned in any year, and the average ROI is significantly below the required return. The conclusion flowing from the price level adjusted accounting information is that the investment should be rejected. But this is inconsistent with the basic economic analysis that indicates that the investment is acceptable.

There are several possible adjustments in the accounting measures to correct the distortion in decision making that currently exists. But the adjustments are not consistent with the measures of income from continuing operations that will be obtained from application of FAS 33 if the investment is undertaken and if the expectations are perfectly realized.

Another possible solution is to prohibit top management from looking at pro forma accounting information prepared in accordance with FAS 33 in deciding whether or not to undertake an investment. This prohibition is not apt to be popular nor could it be enforced. An easier solution is to recognize that price level accounting will not have a one-to-one relationship with investment decision making. An investment showing a less than acceptable real return on investment may still be desirable.

In the above example one cause of difficulty in the use of the data is that the monetary gains from the outstanding debt are omitted. But we could redescribe the financing to be all common stock and eliminate all monetary gains and still have the difficulty that an investment yielding a .20 internal rate of return is declared to be unacceptable when the required return is .18 if the price level adjusted cash flow measures (constant dollars) are used to determine the acceptability of the investment. In the above example the projected cash flows were based on the forecasted inflation rate (the inflation was perfectly predicted).

In the example the conventional accounting measure indicates the investment is acceptable. While it is true that in another situation there can also be problems with the unadjusted measure of income, conventional accounting at least bypasses some of the distortions of the price level adjustment measure when the inflation has been predicted.

Price Level Adjustment and Taxation

It is likely that a large part of the motivation for price level accounting does not come from a desire to improve financial accounting, but rather from a desire to modify the tax law and to control inflation. For example, R. G. Nichols writes:[2]

> We at Price Waterhouse believe that the impact of inflation should appear as a last and separate one-line item, immediately following conventionally determined net income, in the primary income statement. By elevating this charge to the primary statements, we believe that the inflationary erosion of capital will be more apropriately highlighted—and the case for tax reform more clear.

Paul McCracken also connects price level accounting and taxation:[3]

> If . . . a strategy for the measurement of profits had been followed during the last decade, corporate earnings would have been closer to the mark. There would not have been the large and capricious rise in the true corporate profit tax rate. And we would be looking at an American economy with far more efficient and technologically advanced production facilities than what we see today.

It is easy to conclude that in its desire to increase the probability of reducing its total tax bill, industry is willing to accept a "second best" method of adjusting financial reporting for inflation. Leaving out the holding gains and losses moves the proposed price level adjustments into a gray area of not being quite correct. There is an incomplete adjustment of a not quite correct (theoretically) nature.

Since World War II the public utility industry has been a prime mover for price level accounting (adjustment of depreciation expense) closely followed by the machine tool industry. Academic accountants have done their share (the present author included) to promote some form of price level accounting, since it is easy to illustrate the deficiencies of adhering to a historical cost system during a period of rapid inflation.

The FASB now requires selected firms to present price level adjusted measures of some expenses, and this is taken by some as

---

[2] R. G. Nichols, "A Dollar Is a Dollar Is a Dollar—but It Clearly Isn't, Isn't, Isn't!" *Dividend,* University of Michigan, Fall 1979, pp. 25–28.

[3] Paul W. McCracken, *FASB Viewpoints,* June 8, 1979, p. 1.

a first step (stumbling though it might be) toward acceptance of price level adjustments.

It is logical to assume that industry hopes that given that one federal agency (the SEC) recognizes the validity of price level adjusted cost, another agency (the Internal Revenue Service), with suitable law changes passed by Congress, will also recognize that historical cost is not a valid basis of computing the expenses of a period.

We want to consider the consequences of price level adjusted depreciation for taxes and to suggest a partial solution of a somewhat different nature.

We will first consider a situation where the price level decreases. Intuition tells us that a firm does not want price level depreciation if prices decrease, and intuition is correct.

With a tax rate of t, and Dep dollars of tax depreciation, the value of the tax deduction is t Dep. If Dep is multiplied by a price level adjustment factor less than 1, the dollar amount of the tax saving is reduced compared to what it would be if historical cost were used.

Thus if a firm were to expect price decreases in the future, it would want to continue using historical cost for tax computation purposes.

However, the economy has had over 40 years of inflation, and it is reasonable to project inflation rather than deflation in the future.

We will consider a sequence of situations where there is inflation. In the first situation we shall see that price level adjusted tax depreciation leads to real gains for the stockholder. In the second situation, the adjustment merely allows the stockholders to maintain their investment.

Assume a situation where the cost of debt is .10, the tax rate is .4, and a firm has the opportunity to invest $1,000 at time zero and earn $1,100 before tax and $1,060 after tax.

Assume the investment is financed completely with debt. With cost based depreciation the firm will generate $1,100 of cash, pay zero taxes, and be able to give the debt holders their required return of .10 ($1,000 of principal and $100 of interest). Thus the stockholders invest nothing and earn nothing.

Now assume there is an 8% inflation and the government allows price level adjusted depreciation. The before tax cash flows are unchanged. The depreciation deduction is now $1,080. Assuming the firm has other taxable income, the tax income is reduced by $80, resulting in an additional tax saving of $32.

Whereas previously the stockholders merely broke even, now with price level adjusted tax depreciation they actually have their financial position improved by the acquisition of a marginal investment.

The reconciling factor is that the bondholders have a fixed dollar claim during a period of inflation. The fixed dollar claim *combined with* price level adjusted tax depreciation allows the stockholders to benefit.

It should be noted that the investment could actually return something less than the required debt flows and still be acceptable.

Price level adjusted tax depreciation expense combined with the use of debt can result in real gains to the common stockholders, in a situation where there would be break-even without inflation and without price level adjustment.

Now let us consider the same asset as described above financed with common stock. The common stockholders will earn .06 after tax with no inflation. With inflation at 8% and no change in the cash flows the stockholders will again earn .06 in money terms, but in real terms they will earn a negative return ($1,060 at the end of the period has less purchasing power than $1,000 at the beginning).

With price level adjusted depreciation of $1,080 and financing by stock the taxable income is $20 and the tax $8. The period 1 cash flow is $1,092 and the stockholders earn .092. If the stockholders wanted a .06 return without inflation, with a .08 inflation it is reasonable to expect the stockholders would want a return larger than .06 + .08. Thus price level adjusted tax depreciation, by itself, will not guarantee a constant real return to stockholders.

One possible solution to the problem of depreciation tax deductions is for the government to allow immediate write-offs of the investment cost. If the cost of an asset is C, the value of the immediate write-off is tC. This will be larger than the present value of conventional tax deductions, but may actually be smaller than the present value of price level adjusted tax deductions.

In fact, the cost of immediate write-off to the government may be less than the cost of conventional tax depreciation plus the 10% investment tax credits. For example, assuming a depreciable life of eight years, the value of the immediate write-off of an asset costing $1,000,000 is $480,000 with a .48 tax rate. The present value of depreciation deductions using SYD method of depreciation and .06 rate of discount is $828,800, and the value of the tax savings is .48 of this, or $398,000. Adding the $100,000 investment tax credit to the $398,000 gives $498,000. As can be seen, the present values are close to being equal. The value of longer-lived assets would be more enhanced by the immediate write-off, since the present value of the tax depreciation deductions is reduced.

In the above example, if the government had a time discount factor of .06, it would prefer the immediate write-off to the use of accelerated depreciation plus a 10% investment tax credit. A corporation with the same time value factor would prefer the depreciation over the immediate write-off, but the preference would switch as the discount rate was raised or the life of the asset was increased.

Average Tax Rates

If the FAS 33 conventions are followed, depreciation expense is adjusted upward and the income is reduced. Since monetary gains are omitted from the income calculation, the effect of applying FAS 33 will be to tend to reduce income. Thus the effective tax rate (the tax expense as a percentage of book income) will be increased compared to the rate obtained using income computed for tax purposes or conventional cost based income. It is felt by some that this information can be used to justify lower tax rates or price level adjusted depreciation expense.

Conclusions

One of the important purposes of FAS 33 is to give managers and analysts an opportunity to learn the pros and cons of price level adjustments. This chapter has emphasized the fact that the "income from continuing operations" prepared on a pro forma basis can lead to distortions in capital budgeting decisons, namely, the rejection of acceptable investments (investments that are desirable from a profit maximizing point of view). Since the income from continuing operations leaves out monetary gains, it is not a comprehensive measure of income and it is not surprising that it is not apt to be consistent with a basic measure of economic desirability such as net present value. The net present value measure more effectively reflects the economic characteristics of the investment than the FAS 33 income measure.

Implicit in the criticism stressed in the chapter is a more general criticism. If an economically desirable investment will result in inferior income measures in each year of life of the asset, are the income measures really useful for evaluating investments? The conclusion would seem to be in the negative.

The price level discussion for financial accounting is confused by the fact that tax considerations (the prospect for change) looms in the background. It is argued here that the effects of price level adjusted tax depreciation are not necessarily going to add to more fairness in the tax structure.

It is suggested that for relatively short-lived assets, say, eight years, the government could allow immediate write-offs and still be better off than with the present arrangements of depreciation expenses plus investment tax credit. The proposed procedure has the virtue of being simpler and more objective than price level adjusted depreciation.

But as we search for a way to improve accounting, David M.

Roderick, chairman of the United States Steel Corporation, perhaps has said best what needs to be done:[4]

> The real need of American business is not another set of figures about price changes; rather, business needs an end to inflation itself. Likewise, the American economy doesn't need just one more index of inflation; it needs a practical and effective means of reducing inflation. . . .

Appendix I to this chapter is an extract from Weyerhaeuser Company's 1979 annual report. It is an excellent summary of one company's valid concerns regarding FAS 33, and effectively reviews the issues discussed in the next chapter.

Key Ideas to Remember

1. FAS 33 type adjustments are not useful for evaluating investment decisions.

2. With FAS 33 type calculations monetary gains and losses do not have to affect the earnings per share figure.

3. With perfectly predicted inflation, price level adjustments may introduce distortion.

4. Inflation reduces the value of the depreciation tax shield.

5. Motivation for price level accounting among business managers to a large extent comes from a desire to see the tax laws changed (see [4] above).

6. The use of price level adjusted depreciation for accounting, but not for tax, will *increase* the effective tax rate (taxes as a percentage of income).

7. A complete price level adjusted accounting system must include monetary gains and losses.

[4]David M. Roderick, *FASB Viewpoints,* June 8, 1979, p. 2.

Appendix I: Extract from Weyerhaeuser Company's 1979 Annual Report

Supplementary financial information

During 1979 the Financial Accounting Standards Board issued Statement No. 33 entitled "Financial Reporting and Changing Prices". The statement requires the presentation of a five-year summary of selected financial information, including data on earnings, sales and other operating revenues, net assets, dividends and market prices per common share. Also required is the presentation of earnings from continuing operations adjusted (a) for the effects of general inflation and (b) to give effect to current costs. A number of preliminary comments and definitions may be useful in understanding better the supplementary financial information presented.

The effects of general inflation are measured by changes in the general purchasing power of the United States dollar as determined by reference to the Consumer Price Index for All Urban Consumers published by the Bureau of Labor Statistics of the U.S. Department of Labor. To give effect to current costs the Company has utilized a number of resources. For product inventories recourse was had to the Company's average replacement cost for the current year. For all other assets required to be restated on a current cost basis reference was made to a number of specific Producer Price Indexes published by the Bureau of Labor Statistics and to the composite Construction Cost Index published by the Department of Commerce. As permitted by Statement No. 33 the Company's timber, timberlands and directly related facilities, for example, logging roads, have been adjusted only for the effects of general inflation. Restatement of these assets on a current cost basis has been deferred pending further study by the Financial Accounting Standards Board.

The supplementary financial information required by Statement No. 33 is limited to presentation of the effects of changing prices on inventory, property and equipment, cost of goods sold, depreciation, amortization and fee stumpage expense. It is only those effects which have been recognized in the required disclosures as to net assets and as to earnings from continuing operations.

The Company believes that the two supplementary earnings computations, one dealing with the effects of general inflation and the other dealing with the effects of specific changes in the prices of resources used by the Company, are apt to be misunderstood and inappropriate conclusions drawn therefrom. Particularly unfortunate, in the view of the Company, is the fact that the disciplines of Statement No. 33 do not deal with the probable effects upon revenues if the Company's costs were, in fact, those costs portrayed in the two supplementary earnings computations, and if the costs of the Company's competitors were similarly and as pervasively affected by changing prices. What has been lost sight of is the observable phenomenon that as, on an industry basis, operating costs rise, revenues must rise to provide an adequate return on invested capital. Although management is obligated to replace assets consumed in the earnings process, that obligation holds only as long as the cost of replacement is justified in terms of reasonably anticipated future, not present, revenues and future, not present, rates of return. U.S. Companies bend to the pressures of competition and delay the imposition of increases in product prices which may in fact be justified on the basis of current costs. The consumer is the beneficiary of pricing based traditonally, to a large extent, on historical cost. Only when operating cost increases pervade an entire industry do operating cost increases, absent governmental intervention, become immediately translatable into revenue increases. If, as the supplementary earnings computations suggest, operating costs on a generalized, industry-pervasive basis increase, then it is likely that, in time, operating revenues, too, would increase. Otherwise, replacement capital could not be found and it is with this matter that Statement No. 33 does not deal. To deal unilaterally with rising costs, however measured, without considering the effect of those rising costs upon revenues and upon earnings were those costs, in fact, to be incurred and be used to measure performance, renders computations so dealing with rising costs suspect and capable of misinterpretation.

Of further concern to the Company is the failure of Statement No. 33 to deal with the earnings aspects of holding assets during periods of changing prices, i.e. holding gains and losses. That such gains and losses do in fact occur is not disputed, but their measurement and classification for financial reporting purposes, in the Company's view, remain issues yet to be satisfactorily resolved.

FOUR

The Use of Replacement Cost

Inflation woes:
Remember when
There used to be
A "Five and Ten"?
Or one cent gum?
A stamp for three?
Or, better yet,
A road map free?
                    FMK

Since the use of a price index implies the use of an average measure of a price change rather than the specific effect on the firm of a change in the price level, some executives look to replacement cost as a solution to the problem of adjusting for price level changes. We argue that if replacement cost is used, it must be used to adjust the balance sheet as well as the income statement. Even then the value gained from reporting replacement cost may well be less than its cost. There are several important limitations to the use of replacement cost.

Portions of this chapter are based on a paper written jointly with Roland E. Dukes titled "Limitations of Replacement Cost" published in *The Quarterly Review of Economics and Business,* Spring 1979, pp. 131–140.

We will consider the use of replacement cost data for the stock of inventory and long-lived assets held by the firm and for the cost of goods sold and depreciation expense for the period of the report.

Meaningful economic interpretations of replacement cost accounting require making assumptions regarding when the replacements will take place, if ever. In order to make the replacement cost data useful to the investor, a great deal of information is necessary. Replacement cost is very difficult to apply.

Financial Accounting

Financial accounting reports are used by a variety of decision makers.

We focus our attention on the investment and credit decisons of financial statement users. More specifically, we limit the discussion to the informational preferences of the investor in the common stock or debt securities of a firm. The investor in the securities of a firm desires information about the profitability and the financial health of the firm.

We assume that a goal of the accounting process is to reflect the economic events that are occurring and to be consistent with them. If the accounting process is consistent with the economic events, then positive income should represent an improvement in financial affairs, and negative income should reflect the fact that at the end of the period the firm is worse off than at the beginning. The terms "improvement in financial affairs" and "worse off" are somewhat ambiguous in this context, but in given situations we can define the terms more precisely. We contend that the accounting income measures should be consistent with the economic changes that take place. It is on this basis that we proceed with an evaluation of the measures of income resulting from the use of replacement cost data.

Consider the accounting income measurement problem for long-lived depreciable assets. The specific issue being addressed is the conditions under which an income number that is derived from using replacement cost information is consistent with the firm (and, therefore, the owners of the firm) being considered better off or worse off as a result of the change in replacement cost.

The basic question to be addressed is whether the firm is better off or worse off when the replacement cost of a long-lived depreciable asset increases. We argue that the presentation of only replacement cost data does not assist in answering this question. On one hand, an increase in replacement cost suggests that the firm is better off in that there is an increase in the recorded basis of an asset and an equal increase in stockholder's equity. The replacement cost also implies a higher periodic depreciation charge than is currently being recorded under historical cost; this suggests that income is being overstated and the firm is worse off than is implied with the historical cost-income number. Although this latter conclusion is incomplete and possibly incorrect, it is freqently highlighted. If there is a positive correlation between replacement costs and current values, the value of the asset will also increase. More information than the direct effect on depreciation expense is required before it is possible to determine whether an increase in replacement cost results in the shareholder being better off or worse off. This same analysis applies if the asset is adjusted using a price index measure.

We analyze replacement cost within the context of the following considerations: (1) replacement cost as an estimation of value, (2) replacement cost and technology changes, (3) replacement cost and replacement timing, and (4) replacement cost as an estimate of the barrier to entry.

An Estimator of Value

Is replacement cost (income based on replacement cost) a reasonable estimator of value (change in value)? Assume the following facts apply to Firms A and B, where for simplicity we assume a world of certainty:

	FIRM A	FIRM B
Original cost of assets	$1,000,000	$1,000,000
Replacement cost of assets	$1,000,000	$3,000,000
Remaining life	10 years	10 years
Replacement cost depreciation	$100,000	$300,000
Income (before depreciation)	$120,000	$200,000
Income (after replacement cost depreciation)	$ 20,000	$100,000 loss

Using the income measure, it would appear that Firm A is to be preferred to Firm B since, all things being equal, $20,000 income is better than a loss of $100,000. However, let us consider the fact that cash flows of $120,000 were earned by Firm A and cash flows of $200,000 were earned by Firm B, and the need for replacement is not expected to take place for 10 years. On a cash flow basis Firm B is preferred (that is, has a greater present value) to Firm A if it is assumed that neither firm replaces in year 10. Thus, if we were to assume that replacement will *not* occur, Firm B with its apparent loss after replacement cost depreciation of $100,000 is preferred to Firm A and its $20,000 income.

Assuming a rate of discount of .10, and no replacement of assets (the firm has a life of 10 years), the economic values of Firms A and B are $737,000 and $1,230,000 respectively. Both values are less than the respective replacement costs of their assets. The present values correctly show that Firm B has a more preferred cash flow than does Firm A; neither the replacement costs nor the income numbers generated using replacement costs reveal this preference.

Why is a replacement cost of $3,000,000 possible in a situation where the cash flows are $200,000 per year? There are several possible explanations. One is that at the time of construction the firm overestimated demand or underestimated expenses. Second, other firms may also have expanded capacity and forced the price down. Third, the cost of replacement may have risen since acquisition of the asset, but the price of the product may have stayed more or less constant. When there is not a high correlation between cash flows and replacement cost, the replacement cost is not a good estimator of value.

In the foregoing example, Firm B has the larger replacement cost and larger present value than Firm A. To show that replacement costs do not necessarily provide the preferred ranking, consider the same example as the foregoing except that the replacement costs are reversed. The cash flows are unchanged. In this case Firm A would have a greater replacement cost than Firm B, but Firm B still has the more preferred cash flows.

In general, replacement cost is not a reliable substitute for value estimators. For example, replacement costs of assets used in the steel industry have increased dramatically, but based on observed market values (and cash flows) one cannot claim an equivalent increase in the values of the assets. In disclosing the required replacement data, many firms are disclaiming that they would ever replace assets in a manner consistent with the procedures used to derive the replacement cost estimates. The disclaimer supports our contentions that the replacement costs do not represent estimates of value for these firms.

It can be argued that the same deficiencies attributed to replacement cost can also be assigned to original cost. Cost based numbers may also not reflect the current values of the assets. It is true that any cost based number will have limited usefulness, since it may not consider the ability of that asset to earn cash flows in the future. However, at the time of purchase the cost is a reasonable estimator of value (the expected value is equal to or greater than cost or the asset would not be purchased).

At time of the replacement cost adjustment there is no reason to assume that values are being measured. The replacement cost is determined by the costs of the factors of production that are inputs into the creation of the asset. The value of the asset is determined by its own physical (economic) characteristics as well as by the supply and demand conditions for the product being produced. There is no reason to think that all these markets are perfectly correlated. The relationship between replacement cost and value is considered further in a later section of this chapter.

In addition, the utilization of replacement cost to adjust depreciation expenses seems to carry an implication that the financial health of a corporation is harmed by an increase in replacement cost. This may not be valid if the cash flows to be earned by the asset are also increasing.

We need to reinforce the point that the following variables are relevant: (1) future costs of replacement (not the present replacement costs), (2) the time at which the replacement takes place (the timing of replacement), and (3) the future cash flows that are expected to take place.

Implicit in this conclusion is the fact that replacement will not take place unless the expected cash flows have increased sufficiently to justify the expenditure of the replacement cost at the time of replacement. The current replacement cost is not relevant unless replacement is going to take place now and a meaningful replacement cost measure can be obtained.

If replacement is going to take place in the future, we can use the current replacement as the basis of estimating the future replacement cost, but there are a number of other possible methods of estimating today what the replacement cost will be at the time of replacement. It is not obvious that the current replacement cost is the best estimator.

Technology Changes

The primary criticism one hears in conversation with managers relating to the use of replacement cost is that technological changes make the estimation of replacement cost irrelevant. If replacement is not to be in kind, of what use is the estimate of replacement cost of assets currently in use?

Defining replacement cost in terms of units of capability or capacity does not help, since the efficiency of new assets would be different. In fact, the preferred method of production that would be installed today might be completely different from that being used currently. There is no easy answer to this criticism.

One solution when there are relatively homogeneous assets is to define replacement cost in terms of prices in the second-hand market for the homogeneous assets. In this situation the replacement cost will reflect changes in technology, since the market price will reflect these changes. On the other hand, many production units have unique characteristics and we must go to the market price for the factors of production or use the market price for unlike units. In these situations it is difficult to define precisely replacement cost in the operational manner.

Timing of Replacement

The timing of the next replacement very much affects the interpretation of the replacement cost information. When replacement cannot or would not take place, the replacement cost information is likely to be close to valueless. The management of the subways of New York City would not find the cost of replacing the tunnels that house the subways to be useful information.

Whether the replacement is discretionary or mandatory and the timing of the replacement are extremely important to the analysis. In the foregoing example, we assumed that replacement was discretionary and we preferred Firm B because of the larger net present value of the cash flows over the next 10 years. Again, assume the situation where Firm A is generating a cash flow of $120,000 and Firm B is generating $200,000 per year. If the replacement is infinitely far away, an investor would prefer Firm B over Firm A, since B's asset has a present value of $(200,000)/r$ compared with $(120,000)/r$ for Firm A, where r is the appropriate time value factor. The replacement cost is irrelevant, since replacement is infinitely far away. The present value of the future cash flows is relevant.

The preference for Firm B is based on the projected cash

flows and the infinitely distant replacement cost does not affect the preference. Not only is the replacement cost irrelevant when the asset has an infinite life, but the infinite life also results in a depreciation charge that should be zero. In this situation, the income of Firm B is equal to its cash flows. In a situation where the replacement is infinitely in the future, the replacement cost is not relevant information to the investor (except as an estimation of the barrier to entry by competitors).

Now consider a situation where replacement cost is imminent. Assume that replacement is to take place immediately and that the assets will again earn cash flows of $120,000 and $200,000 per year for Firms A and B respectively. Assume the lives of the new assets will be infinite. With a 10% rate of discount Firm A would invest (the net present value is $200,000), but Firm B has no economic incentive to invest $3,000,000 to earn $200,000 per year with a 10% rate of discount.

Firm B is not a desirable alternative *if* it had to replace its asset immediately with no change in the price of the output. Firm B is desirable if replacement is infinitely far in the future, but not desirable if replacement is immediate. There is a switch point where B moves from undesirable to desirable as we move the replacement time out (the switch point with one replacement cycle is a little over four years).

Thus the timing of asset replacement moved our preference from Firm B (with no replacement pending) to Firm A (with immediate replacement). In fact, by moving the date of asset replacement for Firm B toward time zero, Firm B becomes an undesirable investment.

The conclusion is that the timing of replacement is valuable information. This implies that while current replacement cost may be an estimator of the expected replacement cost at the time of replacement, this latter number is of more relevance. To present the current replacement cost without information about the timing of replacement and the estimated cost of replacement at that time may be misleading.

A second important piece of information is whether or not

the replacement is discretionary. With discretionary replacement we can assume that replacement will take place only if the present value of the expected cash flows exceeds the replacement cost. Both the revenues and the expenses will be relevant to the analysis.

For example, now consider a situation where replacement is to take place in 10 years but the replacement will be completely optional with either firm able to cease operations. Since Firm B will earn $200,000 a year for the next 10 years compared with $120,000 a year for Firm A, at the same purchase price for either firm an investor considering only the first 10 years will prefer Firm B. Firm B will accumulate more cash over the 10-year period than Firm A and replacement is optional.

If at the end of 10 years both firms *had* to replace and we assume uncertainty, then it is no longer obvious as to whether one would prefer A or B. The relative desirability of the two firms now will depend on the expected replacement costs and the forecast cash flows on the investments at time 10, but Firm B definitely decreases in desirability if the expected replacement cost is $3,000,000.

Consider two firms which are identical except for replacement timing, and where the positive cash flows are not affected by the timing of the replacement. If one firm has a replacement cost of R at time 10, then $R (1 + r)^{-10}$ should be subtracted from its present value. If the second firm has its replacement at time zero, then R_0 should be subtracted from its present value where R_0 is the current replacement cost. The resulting net present values of the two firms is likely to differ.

In a situation where the replacement cost is currently high (and a loss appears after deducting replacement cost depreciation), the firm may be a desirable investment as long as the replacement is reasonably distant, or the firm has an option to withdraw from the activity. If investments are optional, any new investment must promise to be sound economically (with large enough future cash flows) or the investment will not be made. The timing of replacement is highly relevant in evaluating replacement cost information.

A Complication

Consider a situation where in any one year only 1% of a fully integrated plant comes up for replacement. There is a tendency to replace piecemeal because otherwise the entire plant has to be shut down. This is different from the already described situations where the replacements were discrete events. Here replacement is continuous.

We used the foregoing example to illustrate the fact that timing of replacement was relevant to economic analysis of the financial affairs of a firm. Continuous replacement does not modify this conclusion about the importance of timing, it merely makes the analysis more complex.

Replacement Cost a Barrier to Entry

Replacement cost is of interest to the extent that it measures the barrier to entry by other firms. If the replacement cost depreciation is accurately measured and leads to a loss, then it may be reasonable to expect that other firms will not be eager to expand productive capacity or to enter the industry. This assumes that the present value analysis accurately reflects the present value of cash flows and technology changes. Thus the replacement costs (if reasonably measured) give some indication of the obstacle facing other firms thinking about entering the game (assuming the technology difficulty is solved).

If reasonable measures of replacement cost can be determined, this information could be very useful to financial statement users as indicators of the difficulty competitors will have to enter the industry. However, it is interesting that the asset replacement cost will probably be at least as important as the replacement cost depreciation expense. It gives an indication of the amount of capital required in today's market to acquire the amount of capacity presently owned by the firm. If the replacement cost measures are reliable, this information would be welcomed by financial analysts for a whole range of purposes, including the acquisition of a firm.

Replacement Cost and Value

While replacement cost is not necessarily a reliable estimator of value, the relationship between increased replacement cost and asset valuation should be considered further. Replacement cost does not determine value, but the relative magnitudes of value and replacement cost provide insights into the economic conditions prevailing in the industry.

If replacement cost is less than the value of the asset (where value is defined in terms of risk adjusted present value), then the industry is not in an equilibrium situation. Capital will be attracted into the industry until replacement cost and value equal. Thus it is possible for replacement cost to be equal to or less than value only for short time periods.

On the other hand, if the value of the asset's product remains unchanged (because of supply and demand conditions) while replacement cost has increased, it is possible for replacement cost to exceed greatly the value of the asset (for example, in the steel industry in 1981). To have replacement cost greater than value is also a disequilibrium situation. We would expect there to be little or no expansion in capacity or even maintenance of present plants. Plants would be shut or allowed to deteriorate until replacement cost and value again were equal. But in the short run it is possible to have replacement cost exceed value.

Thus while replacement cost does not affect value directly, the investment cost (or equivalently the cost of capacity) will affect the amount of investment that will take place and will indirectly affect the value of the assets. For example, if investment cost exceeds value, ultimately shortage of supply will tend to cause the price of the product to increase, thus increasing the value of the remaining assets.

Conclusions

Replacement cost information is of limited usefulness when it is not supplemented with additional data regarding when the assets of the firm are expected to be replaced, as well as the degree of discretion available to management as to whether the assets are replaced. The replacement cost data for a reasonably new hotel have economic significance different from the replacement cost information about a 10-year-old taxicab. Both are different in significance from the replacement cost of a fleet of 747, 707, and 727 airplanes purchased over the past 20 years. Changing technologies and the timing of replacement all affect the interpretation of the data.

If a user of financial information is informed only of the replacement cost of assets that have been expensed during the period, very little useful information has been provided. The user will not know whether a loss with replacement cost indicates that the firm is worthless (assuming no changes in the future) as in Firm B's immediate replacement case, or whether the loss is essentially meaningless because replacement is in the distant future.

It is important to keep in mind that an increase in replacement costs increases assets and stockholders' equity (both increases are desirable) as well as increasing expense (which is undesirable). The conclusion as to whether a change in replacement cost results in the firm being better or worse off is much more complex than merely noting the direct income statement effect.

Unless very complete and useful replacement cost information is to be presented (and admittedly, this would be difficult to obtain), we question whether the benefits achieved with the partial replacement cost data in published statements are greater than the real costs of accumulating the information. We conclude that the costs of obtaining the information are likely to be larger than the expected value of the information. Without making extensive and important assumptions regarding the timing of replacement, we see no way that an investor can effectively use raw replacement cost data.

Many of the same problems of applying replacement cost accounting also apply when price indexes are used. Inflation results in increased price level adjusted depreciation expense, but the plant assets and stockholders' equity are also increased by the use of the price index.

Selected Bibliography

KLAASEN, JAN, "Current Replacement Value Accounting in Western Europe," *Current Replacement Cost: An International Perspective, A Symposium Presented by the Department of Accounting* (Stillwater: Oklahoma State University, 1976).

REVSINE, LAWRENCE, *Replacement Cost Accounting* (Englewood Cliffs, N.J.: Prentice-Hall, 1973).

Financial Accounting Standards Board, *Objectives of Financial Reporting and Elements of Financial Statements of Business Enterprises: A Proposed Statement of Financial Accounting Concepts (Stamford, Conn.: 1977).*

U.S. Securities and Exchange Commission, *Accounting Series Release No. 190* (ASR 190) (Washington, 1976).

Key Ideas to Remember

1. The relevance of replacement cost accounting depends on when, if ever, the replacement will take place.

2. Replacement cost may not be a good estimate of the value of an asset.

3. Assuming modest technology change, replacement cost is an estimate of the barrier to a competitor wanting to enter the industry.

4. Replacement cost information is of limited usefulness.

5. Replacement cost of an asset that will not be replaced is not relevant for decision making.

6. The use of replacement cost information which contains a high level of subjectivity is a poor substitute for value estimators, which also contain a high level of subjectivity.

FIVE

Inflation and the Use of Debt

Inflation makes the debtor's world
Look cheerful, bright, and sunny
As the firm pays back its creditors
Using cheaper money.

On the other hand the creditor
Is cross and discontent
For the buying power of what's paid back
Is far less than was lent.

FMK

Conventional wisdom says that debt should be used to increase profits if inflation is anticipated. Borrow $1,000 when the price index is 100 and you will only owe $800 in dollars of equivalent purchasing power when the price index is 125. The $200 monetary gain is the motivation for using the debt. This analysis is correct but incomplete. More analysis is necessary before a conclusion can be reached as to the desirability of issuing debt.

If the $1,000 of debt capital is invested in land worth $1,000 at the beginning of the period and $1,250 at the end, the desirability of the debt is emphasized, but we still cannot reach a conclusion until we have more information than is presented above.

By now you might have noticed one significant omission from the analysis. We have not indicated the amount of interest (or rate of interest) that has to be paid by the borrowing corpora-

57

tion. This information is required before a decision can be made.

Now we are ready for a theoretically correct conclusion concerning the use of debt during inflation. Debt may be desirable, but the desirability of issuing debt will depend on the relative cost of debt and other securities, and the availability of debt capital compared to the availability of other types of capital. Finally, the cost of debt must be compared to the return that can be earned on an investment, and changes in risk must be considered before it is decided that the acquisition of an asset financed by debt is desirable.

Whether or not debt has a real cost and the magnitude of the real cost will depend on the relative size of the interest cost compared to the inflation rate.

We want to explain the effect of inflation on gains and losses of being in debt (short or long term), and to investigate how the cost of debt should be evaluated when there are interest rate changes as well as price level changes.

We will first consider the situation where inflation is perfectly anticipated by the market and the interest rate reflects this situation (there is an equilibrium situation).

Perfectly Anticipated Inflation

Let us assume a situation where the inflation rate is j and the money market with zero inflation would require a return of r. The nominal interest rate k gives a return $(1 + k)$ which when deflated by the inflation factor $(1 + j)$ offers a real return of $1 + r$. Expressed algebraically, we have:

$$\frac{1 + k}{1 + j} = 1 + r$$

Solving for k:

$$k = r + j + rj$$

Not only do we assume that the inflation is perfectly anticipated, but in addition it is assumed that the investor has investment opportunities that yield a real return of r; thus the investor is able to demand an equivalent nominal return of k.

Assume the required real return is .05 and the inflation rate is .20. Thus $r = .05$, $j = .20$, and we have for the required nominal return k:

$$k = .05 + .20 + .01 = .26$$

For example, a one-period $1,000 debt will have to pay .26 interest, or $260, at time 1 for the investor to earn a real return of .05. The issuing firm will incur the following costs:

Interest cost	$260
Less monetary gain on $1,000 of debt	200
Net real cost in end of period dollars	$ 60

In terms of beginning of the year dollars the real cost is $60/1.20 = $50, or .05 on the $1,000 of initial debt. The real cost is .05.

The investor lending $1,000 at time zero receives at time 1 $1,260. In terms of beginning of the year dollars this is: $1,260/1.20 = $1,050, which is a .05 real return on an investment of $1,000.

A constant dollar accounting procedure for the issuer of the debt or an economic analysis of the costs and gains would report a monetary gain of $200 associated with the $1,000 debt, but the inflated interest cost of $260 would balance out the monetary gain and result in a net cost of $60. With perfectly anticipated inflation a firm would not necessarily borrow funds because of inflation, since the inflation factor is fully incorporated into the interest rate that borrowers demand (there may be other reasons for borrowing). But if the actual inflation rate is not equal to the projected inflation rate, then a gain or loss may be incurred.

With no inflation we would expect to pay a real cost of .05 for debt. With a .20 inflation we would expect to pay a nominal cost of .26 and the real cost is again .05.

We will now expand the example to examine a relatively long-

term monetary debt situation. Consider a three-year debt paying
.26 per year where the facts are as described above (r = .05,
j = .20). Table 5-1 shows the issuing firm's results for each of the
three years assuming the debt size stays constant at $1,000.

Table 5-1 shows that the net real cost for each year is a constant $50, and this is unchanged from the one-period example.
The real cost of the debt is .05 for each year.

If, instead of a bond, we had a constant payment to amortize
the $1,000 debt (say $519.91 payment per year) costing .26, the
analysis would be similar, though the numbers would change.
Table 5-2 shows the conventional debt amortization schedule for
the equal payment debt paying .26 interest.

Table 5-3 shows the computation of the net real cost for each
year.

Table 5-3 (and its footnotes) shows that the net real cost is
exactly equal to .05 of the debt where the debt cost is computed to
include the monetary gain. The time to maturity of the debt or the
nature and timing of the payments do not affect the basic interpretation of the net real cost of having debt outstanding.

TABLE 5-1.   Three-Year Bond

Year	Interest Cost	Monetary Gain	Net Real Cost (Beginning of Period Dollars)
1	260	200	60/1.20 = 50
2	260	200	60/1.20 = 50
3	260	200	60/1.20 = 50

TABLE 5-2.   Debt Amortization Schedule

Year	Beginning Balance	Interest (.26)	Payment
1	1,000.00	260.00	519.91
2	740.09	192.42	519.91
3	412.60	107.28	519.91

TABLE 5-3. Three-Year Debt: Equal Payments

Year	Col. 1 Beginning Balance	Col. 2 Interest Cost	Col. 3 Monetary Gain	Col. 4 Net Real Cost (End of Period Dollars)	Col. 5 $\left(\dfrac{\text{Col. 4}}{1.20}\right)$ Beginning Dollars	Col. 6 $\left(\dfrac{\text{Col. 5}}{\text{Col. 1}}\right)$ Real Cost
1	1,000	260	200	60*	50	.05
2	740	192	148	44**	36.7	.05
3	413	107	83	24***	20	.05

*(1,000 + 200) .05 = 60
**(740 + 148) .05 = 44
***(413 + 83) .05 = 24

61

Unanticipated Inflation

To this point we have defined j as both the actual and anticipated
rates of inflation. Now we will assume the actual rate of inflation
is not necessarily equal to the anticipated rate. This will cause the
actual monetary gain from inflation to differ from the anticipated. For example, assume the actual rate of inflation for
each year of the situation described in Table 5–3 to be .10 instead
of the .20 that was forecast by the market. We would then have
the results from inflation and operations as shown in Table 5–4.
The debt payment is $519.91 each year (see Table 5–2).

The net real cost is now higher than that shown in Table 5–3
because the inflation rate is now less than the assumed inflation
incorporated in the nominal interest rate. If the actual inflation
rate had been higher than the .20 that was forecast (say .40), the
net real cost would have been lower than that in Table 5–3 or 5–4.

Instead of assuming that the forecast inflation rate was not
realized, we can assume that there is not equilibrium. That is, k is
not equal to r + j + rj. For example, assume investors want a
real return of .05 and the inflation rate is .20. The investors want a
nominal return of .26, but debt is yielding .20. In this situation the
real return is zero, not the .05 desired by the investors. The real
cost to the corporation is zero, even though it is paying .20 in
nominal terms.

Why do investors buy a security with a zero or negative real

TABLE 5–4.   Unanticipated Inflation (a .10 Rate)
(Continuing the Basic Situation of Table 5–3)

Year	Beginning Balance	Interest Cost	Actual Monetary Gain	Net Real Cost	Real Cost
1	1,000	260	100	160	.16
2	740	192	74	118	.16
3	413	107	41	66	.16

return? If this is the best investment alternative, then the security will be purchased, even though the real return is zero or negative. But if the situation persists where debt securities have a negative real return, we can expect investors to shift into real assets that have the potential of at least keeping up with inflation (not having a negative return).

Assume the debt interest rate is lower than an equilibrium interest rate. We can expect to see debt holders requiring the potential for gains in excess of the explicit interest rate being charged. Some home mortgages now have the lender sharing in any gain on sale. Corporate debt sometimes offers the possibility of the lenders sharing in the profits if the profits exceed a given number of dollars. A more common situation is where the debt is convertible into common stock or the lender receives detachable warrants as well as the conventional contractual cash flows.

Is an interest cost high? Assume a long-term interest rate of .15 for a triple B rated debt. This is a high rate on historical basis (compared to rates charged in the past). But given an inflation rate of .15 and the forecast of continued inflation in the future, the real interest cost is much less than .15. In fact with an inflation rate of .15 the real cost is zero. If the inflation rate is .16, the real cost would be negative. We would expect the real cost of triple A rated debt to have even a lower real cost.

Example

Compute the real cost of borrowing if the inflation rate is .12 and the nominal interest rate is .15.

We know that $j = .12$ and $k = .15$. Since:

$$k = r + j + rj$$

we can solve for r. We have:

$$r = \frac{k - j}{1 + j} = \frac{.15 - .12}{1.12} = .028$$

Up to this point, we have assumed that the interest rates did not change through time. Constant dollar accounting focuses on purchasing power changes and tends to ignore other value changes that take place. In this section we will consider both purchasing power effects and changing interest rates.

Consider the conventional bond paying .26 that results in Table 5-1. At time zero the discount rate being used to evaluate the bond is .26 and the present value of the bond is $1,000.

If after one time period at time 1 the one-period interest rate for period 2 is .30 and for period 3 is .20, the present value of the debt at time 1 is $1,080. We will assume the bond is not callable. If B_1 is the value of the bond at time 1:

$$B_1 = \frac{260}{1.30} + \frac{1,260}{(1.30)(1.20)} = 1,080$$

If at time 2 the one-period interest rate for period 3 is .10, the value of the bond at time 2 is:

$$B_2 = \frac{1,260}{1.10} = 1,145$$

The changing interest rates cause changes in the value of the bond.

The gains and losses to the corporate issuer from the changes in interest rates are:

PERIOD	GAIN OR LOSS FROM INTEREST RATE CHANGES
1	$B_0 - B_1 = 1,000 - 1,080 = $ 80 loss
2	$B_1 - B_2 = 1,080 - 1,145 = $ 65 loss
3	$B_2 - B_3 = 1,145 - 1,000 = $ 145 gain

If the price level were constant, the above table would still show the gains and losses arising from interest rate changes. But assume the inflation rate of period 1 is .30, of period 2 is .25, and of period 3 is .15.

The monetary gains are:

TABLE 5–5. Monetary Gains from Debt

Period	COL. 1 *Present Value of Debt (Beginning of Period)*	COL. 2 *Actual Inflation Rate*	COL. 3 (COL. 1 × COL. 2) *Monetary Gain*
1	1,000	.30	300
2	1,080	.25	270
3	1,145	.15	172

Putting all the above information together we obtain Table 5–6:

TABLE 5–6. Changing Interest Rates and Inflation Rates

Period	COL. 1 *Interest Cost*	COL. 2 *Monetary Gain*	COL. 3 *Loss (Gain) from Interest Rate Change*	COL. 4 (1 + 3 − 2) *Net Real Cost*
1	260	300	80	40
2	260	270	65	55
3	260	172	(145)	− 57

If the actual inflation rate equaled the anticipated rate and if the interest rate changes were ignored, the monetary gains of each period would be equal to $200. If we recognize the changing value of the debt because of interest rate changes, the monetary gains of the periods would differ from those obtained using $1,000 as the base of the monetary gain calculation because the beginning of the period debt differs each period.

Conclusions

If price level adjustments are made for accounting purposes, we can expect there to be differences of opinion about whether or not the gains and losses associated with monetary assets and liabilities are relevant. While one has to be careful in interpreting the significance of the gains and losses, this chapter has shown how, with perfectly anticipated inflation, the recognition of the monetary gains from being in debt merely reduces the interest cost to a net real cost. If one is interested in the real cost of debt, monetary gains on liabilities should be recognized in the period in which the change in price level occurs. This conclusion is not altered by shifting from single-period to multiperiod debt.

The second point illustrated in this chapter is a combination of constant dollar and value measurement as it applies to debt. While initially we can expect that inflation but not interest rate changes will be considered, in the long run some type of value accounting is inevitable. A relatively simple adjustment enables us to compute not only the monetary gain but also the change in debt value that arises from the change in interest rates. This loss or gain reflects the fact (in the example) that the option of retiring the debt at the market price would now cost more or less than previously and that the current contracts have increased or decreased in terms of present value.

The easy generalizations about the use of debt during inflation are not valid. We can only conclude that debt is desirable after detailed analyses of the costs and benefits of using debt. Debt costing .18 is cheap if the inflation rate is .20 and if investments yielding .25 are available. The real cost of debt is negative if the inflation rate is larger than the nominal interest rate. In Chapter 12 we will consider the effect of taxes on the cost of debt.

Key Ideas to Remember

1. We cannot conclude without analysis that debt is desirable during an inflationary period.

2. It is important to distinguish between real and nominal interest costs.

3. The term structure of interest rates (different rates for different time periods) affects decisions.

4. The real cost of debt can be negative even when the nominal cost is at a historical high.

5. Even where we can conclude the debt is desirable, it is possible that some other form of capital is even more desirable.

6. The conventional wisdom that a firm should use more debt during inflation may or may not be correct in a specific situation.

SIX

Price Level Accounting and Stock Valuation

Don't store your money in the bank—
Its worth falls with inflation.
Common stock at very best
Bears close examination.
And I know financial types
Will cringe and make loud static
Should I suggest you take your cash
And hide it in the attic.
It doesn't pay to keep your wealth.
It doesn't pay to lend it.
So when all is said and done—
Oh joy!—we'll have to spend it!*

* My purchases were not as planned—
The Grim Accountant says, "Buy land!"
                                        FMK

One function of accounting is to supply information that can then be used by investors in the valuation of common stock. This chapter will consider the usefulness of conventional accounting and price level adjusted accounting relative to this one function.

There are many examples in the finance literature of interest in price level accounting. For example Davidson, Skelton, and Weil (3) (see References at end of this chapter) estimate the effect of applying price level adjustments to 30 Dow Jones industrial companies. Modigliani and Cohn (5) use price level adjusted data to show the stock market was undervalued (in 1977) by 50%. Obviously, a better understanding of the effects of adjusting and not adjusting for price level changes is desirable.

Since we will assume certainty, the stock value will be computable. The stock value will be defined as being equal to the present value of future dividends. Both the balance sheet and the income statement based measures of stock equity will be compared to the theoretically computed stock value.

We will first consider a firm with only monetary assets and then a firm with real assets with a perpetual life. Finally we will consider a firm with finite-lived real assets.

The Statement of Financial Accounting Standards No. 33 of the FASB defines a method of financial reporting for changing prices. The procedures of this chapter could be reconciled to those of FAS 33 if the monetary gains and losses were excluded in the calculation of the period's earnings per share. Since they are included here in the income measures the results of FAS 33 are inconsistent with the price level adjustments of this chapter. The objective is to illustrate the uses and limitations of price level adjustments for common stock valuation.

Monetary Assets: One Year

Assume a firm has $1,000 of cash financed by common stock at both the beginning and the end of the year. An investor would be willing to pay as much as $1,000 for the firm at the beginning of the year (assuming the firm can be liquidated). With no transactions the firm would have a $200 monetary loss for the year and the two price level adjusted balance sheets would be:

	Beginning of Year	*End of Year*
Cash	1,200	1,000
Stock equity	1,200	1,000

The above balance sheets have all items expressed in year end purchasing power.

The company has a $200 loss, but if the company can be liquidated the stock is again worth $1,000 at year end. The loss in purchasing power reflects a real change, but the common stock price is set in monetary terms, so the year end price does not change compared to the beginning of the year price. There is a change in real value.

The year end balance sheets using conventional accounting and using price level accounting are identical. They are equally useful when all assets are monetary in nature. The price level accounting better shows the erosion in value taking place from the beginning of the period to the end. But for purposes of common stock valuation the statements of financial position are equally useful.

The price level accounting statements are very useful if the objective is to determine whether a firm is better off at the end of the period than at the beginning. For common stock valuation they are much less useful. The income statement is apt to be misleading, for purposes of common stock valuation, if the future flows can be changed by a decision. Errors in evaluation are likely if monetary losses are included, and if the analyst is not very sophisticated relative to the use of price level adjusted data. FAS 33 excludes monetary gains and losses from the calculation of earnings per share, but this is no guarantee of useful information.

The above example considered only one period. The analysis is modified if we switch to considering a perpetual stream.

Monetary Assets: Infinite Life

We will make the assumption that at time zero the accounting measures of the asset and liability are equal to their market values. There will be no changes in interest rates (a change in interest rates would require a change in asset and liability values).

At time zero the stock value is equal to:

$$S = A - L$$

where:

A = monetary assets
L = liabilities

Assume that the monetary assets earn a nominal return of .26. The price level increases by .20. The real interest rate is .05. The debt costs .26. This is an equilibrium relationship. That is:

$$k = .05 + .20 + (.05)(.20) = .26$$

Since there is no risk, the stockholders require the same .26 nominal return as the debt holders.

The conventional balance sheets and income statement are:

	0	*1 (Before Dividend)*	*1 (After Dividend)*
A	100	105.20	100
L	80	80.00	80
S	20	25.20	20
Income before interest			26.00
Interest			20.80
Income			5.20

Assume the $5.20 income is paid as a dividend when received. After the dividend, the end of the period monetary measures are the same as the measures at the beginning of the year. The $5.20 of net income (dividends) is then a perpetuity. The present value of the common stock at time zero is $20 if .26 is used as the discount rate:

$$P = \frac{5.20}{.26} = \$20$$

The above calculation of $20 value is the present value of both income and dividends, since there is no retention of earnings. Both the balance sheet and the income statement using conventional accounting are reasonable representations of stock equity value for the example. No price level adjustments are necessary to value the common stock with a monetary asset.

Adjusting to end of the period dollars, the price level adjusted statement (before the dividend) for the first time period is:

	0	1 (Before Dividend)	
A	120	105.20	20 loss (equal to 120 + 5.20 − 105.20)
L	96	80	16 gain (equal to 96 − 80)
S	24	25.20	1.20 increase

Operating income	$ 5.20
Asset: monetary loss	20.00
Debt: monetary gain	16.00
Income	1.20

The price level adjustments implicitly assume all the transactions take place at time 1.

Despite there only being $1.20 of price adjusted income, there is $5.20 available for dividends. The present value of the dividend stream is unchanged from that previously computed:

$$P = \frac{5.20}{.26} = \$20$$

A stock price of $20 at time zero is consistent with the present value of the dividends and the recorded (cost based) stock value. The $24 of stockholders' equity at time zero shown above is in end of the period dollars. Adjusted to beginning of the period dollars we have $24/1.20 = $20.

The price level adjusted income including monetary gains and losses is $1.20. The present value of a perpetuity of $1.20 discounted at .05 is:

$$P = \frac{1.20}{.05} = \$24$$

Discounting the real income perpetuity of $1.20 by the real

interest rate of .05 gives $24, the beginning value in terms of year end dollars. In beginning of the period dollars the value is again $20.

The price level adjusted accounting is a reasonable basis for stock valuation of an all monetary asset firm offering a stream of perpetual earnings if the monetary gains and losses are included in the income measure. Both conventional accounting and price level adjusted accounting give good estimates of value. But note that the price level adjusted income was discounted using the real interest rate of .05 and not the nominal rate of .26.

One has to be careful in defining the revenue stream of the monetary asset. We assumed a constant revenue of $26 per period. The real value of this stream then decreased through time. A different revenue stream could conceivably convert the monetary asset into being the economic equivalent of a real asset, thus requiring different adjustments.

Also, the example started with the asset and liability recorded using conventional accounting where the conventional measure was equal to a value measure. If there had been bad initial conventional accounting, we would have had bad price level accounting. The same conclusion is valid if at any time after time zero the economic environment changes so that the conventional accounting no longer measures the value of the asset. The conventional accounting does not show the erosion in purchasing power, but it does supply sufficient information for stock valuation if all the assets are monetary in nature.

Real Assets: Perpetual Life

We will now assume that all the firm's assets are real with a perpetual life and they increase in dollar value consistent with the inflation rate so that the real value stays constant. With a .20 inflation rate the assets increase in dollar value by .20. The before interest income each period increases by .20. Assume a $100 asset is financed of $80 debt and $20 stock.

We again assume an inflation rate of .20, a real borrowing rate of .05, and a nominal borrowing rate of .26:

$$k = .05 + .20 + (.05)(.20) = .26$$

Any cash generated after interest payments will be paid as a dividend.

We will assume the initial liability of $80 will increase in monetary terms by .20 per year. The increase in the liability is being used to pay part of the interest each year (a discount bond is one method of accomplishing this). The capital structure is being kept constant in real terms.

The first year's interest expense is .26 × $80 = $20.80, the net interest payment in year 1 is $4.80, and the increase in the liability the first year is $16. The interest payments increase by .20 per year, since the liability increases by .20. The interest payment in year 2 is $5.76 and in year 3 is $6.912.

Assume the first year's income before the interest is $6 received at the end of the year. The income increases by .20 each year.

The before interest incomes (this implicitly assumes the revenues and expenses increase proportionately with inflation), the payments of interest, and the dividends of each year are:

	1	2	3
Income before interest	6.00	7.20	8.640
Payments of interest	4.80	5.76	6.912
Dividends	1.20	1.44	1.728

The present value of the before interest incomes for an infinite time period using .26 as the discount rate and a .20 growth rate is $100:

$$P = \frac{6}{.26 - .20} = \$100$$

This $100 is a reasonable value measure, and it is based on convential accounting and the use of the nominal interest rate.

The actual interest expense of year 1 is \$20.80 (that is, .26 × \$80); the actual interest paid is \$4.80 and the liability increases by \$16 to \$96. The dividend of year 1 is \$1.20.

In year 1 the income after interest expense of \$20.80 is a loss of \$14.80. Adding the \$1.20 of dividends, the decrease in retained earnings is \$16.00.

Conventional accounting would show the following balance sheets:

	0	*1*	*2*	*3*
A	100	100	100.00	100.00
L	80	96	115.20	138.24
S	20	4	− 15.20	− 38.24

It appears that the debt is becoming too large and the dividend policy should be changed. This is misleading. The income before interest is increasing at a rate of .20 per year, so will be sufficient to pay the interest, which is also increasing at a rate of .20.

Since conventional accounting records the asset at cost, it fails to recognize the increased dollar value of the asset and understates the stockholder's equity. The balance sheets based on conventional accounting are deficient when the firm has real assets with the characteristic of having increasing cash flows through time.

We are assuming that the cash flow (income) generated by the assets starts at \$6 and increases at the inflation rate. The interest payment starts at \$4.80 and increases by .20 per year. Even if all the \$20.80 of interest expense were to be paid in period 1, an amount equal to \$16 would have to be borrowed in order to pay it, so the situation would be unchanged from that presented. The liability would still increase by \$16 in period 1 if the dividend policy is unchanged (a dividend of \$1.20 is paid at time 1).

At time zero the stock has a value of \$20 (the present value of \$100 minus the liability of \$80 or the present value of the dividends starting at\$1.20 growing at .20 and discounted at .26):

$$P = \frac{1.20}{.26 - .20} = \$20$$

The conventional accounting balance sheet is useful at time zero but at any other time it is misleading. For example, showing the asset at $100 at time 3 is misleading when the value of the asset is $172.80.

While examples can be prepared where conventional accounting is consistent with value measures, in this type of situation (a real asset paying an increasing cash flow each year) the conventional accounting measures of financial position fail. The increase in the value of the asset is not recorded. There is no depreciation expense, since the asset increases in value each year. The successive year end price level adjusted balance sheets (each in different year end purchasing power) are:

	0	1	2	3
A	100	120	144.00	172.80
L	80	96	115.20	138.24
S	20	24	28.80	34.56

The price level adjusted balance sheets for time zero and time 1, at time 1 in time 1 dollars, after the $1.20 dividend, are:

	0	1
A	120	120
L	96	96
S	24	24

The price level adjusted income for period 1 is:

Income before interest		6.00
Interest payment	4.80	
Interest accrual	16.00	20.80
Loss		14.80
Monetary gain on the beginning debt of $80		16.00
Net income		1.20
Dividend		1.20
Change in stock equity		0

Each pair of balance sheets for a given year (the beginning and ending financial positions) will be identical, reflecting the fact that no real changes are taking place given the dividend payments. The numbers will change for the different years, but the beginning and ending balances will be equal for each year.

The first year's income before interest using conventional accounting is $6.00 with interest expense of $20.80 and the payment of interest of $4.80. The $6 received at time 1 deflated by .20 inflation is $5, so that the asset is earning $5 real in beginning dollars. The next year's earnings are $7.20, which again deflates to $7.20/(1.20 × 1.20) = $5 real. In fact each year's income deflates to $5 real (beginning of period zero dollars). The present value of a $5 perpetuity is $100 using a .05 real discount factor. Note that the real incomes of $5 per period must be discounted using a real interest rate.

The real income after interest and monetary gains for each year is $1.20 in terms of end of year 1 dollars. If we assume a perpetuity of $1 real incomes in beginning of the year dollars discounted at the real interest rate of .05, we would obtain a $20 present value for the stock equity. The $20 can also be obtained discounting the dividends of $1.20, $1.44, $1.728, etc., by .26:

$$P = \frac{D}{k - g} = \frac{1.20}{.26 - .20} = \$20$$

where .20 is the growth rate in dividends.

If the real asset had been financed entirely with stock equity capital, the analysis would be simpler. Dividends would increase by .20 per year. The conventional accounting would show the same balance sheet each period:

$$
\begin{array}{ll}
A & 100 \\
S & 100
\end{array}
$$

and the income statement would show incomes and dividends of $6, $7.20, $8.60, etc., for successive years with a present value of $100 using .26 as the discount rate:

$$P = \frac{6}{.26 - .20} = \$100$$

The price level adjusted balance sheets each year would be different, but at the end of each year the beginning and ending balances would be the same. Analogously, the income for a year measured in year end dollars of that year will increase by .20 per year, but the real income converted into time zero purchasing power will be $5, with a present value of $100 using the .05 interest rate.

If there are real assets with increasing monetary value, the price level adjusted information is superior to the conventional balance sheet measures.

Real Asset: Finite-lived

Once we shift to considering finite-lived real assets, anything is possible. Conventional accounting may be better than price level adjusted, but we do not know until the facts have been investigated.

Assume that a firm's assets costing $3,000 will generate the following cash flows:

1	1,780
2	1,520
3	1,260

The asset is recorded at its cost of $3,000, and the firm uses straight line depreciation. Only stock equity capital is being used to finance the asset.

This is a special example, but it illustrates a more general problem in the use of price level adjustments.

We again assume a .20 inflation rate, a .05 real interest, and a .26 time value factor. The cash flows after time zero are all paid out as dividends. The conventional balance sheets using straight line depreciation are:

Time

	0	1	2	3
Assets	3,000	2,000	1,000	0
Stock equity	3,000	2,000	1,000	0

The income statements of each year are:

	1	2	3
Revenue	1,780	1,520	1,260
Depreciation	1,000	1,000	1,000
Income	780	520	260

Because the asset has finite life and the incomes are not equal to the cash flows, we cannot use the present value of the incomes to determine the value of the stock. In this specific example the present values of the dividends at the three different moments in time are equal to the conventional accounting measures of stock equity:

$$P_0 = \frac{1,780}{1.26} + \frac{1,520}{(1.26)^2} + \frac{1,260}{(1.26)^3} = 3,000$$

$$P_1 = \frac{1,520}{1.26} + \frac{1,260}{(1.26)^2} = 2,000$$

$$P_2 = \frac{1,260}{1.26} = 1,000$$

$$P_3 = 0$$

If we were to use the incomes to compute the present value at the common stock, we would have to subtract the .26 cost of the capital being used and add the present values of the incomes after the .26 capital cost (the incomes are zero in this case) to the $3,000 recorded cost of the asset. This present value measure of value is consistent with the present value measure obtained using the cash flows.

If we adjust for price level, the balance sheets for the first two time periods using time 1 purchasing power become:

	0	1
Assets	3,600	2,400
Stock equity	3,600	2,400

Since there are no monetary assets or liabilities, the income statement with depreciation price level adjusted is:

Revenue	1,780
Depreciation	1,200
Income	580
Dividend	1,780
Change in stock equity (decrease)	(1,200)

Indicating a value of $2,400 at time 1 ($2,000 × 1.20) is misleading, since the present value of the asset at time 1 is $2,000. The situation being illustrated is analogous to a situation where the forecast of inflation is perfect. There are no surprises. Adjusting for price level in this specific situation is misleading, since the real asset is analogous to a monetary asset when there is perfectly forecast inflation.

Assuming Replacement

Now we will assume that after three periods the asset will have to be replaced. Because of .20 inflation per year the cost of the replacement at time 3 will have risen to $5,184:

$$3,000 \ (1.20)^3 = \$5,184$$

Assume the investment is marginally desirable (earns .26) with the following cash flows:

TIME	CASH FLOWS
0	− 5,184
1	+ 3,075.84
2	+ 2,626.56
3	+ 2,177.28

If the asset earned any less than the cash flows shown, the present asset should not be replaced.

The existence of this asset with an inflated cost should not affect the accounting for the basic investment costing $3,000. If the forecast is correct, the new asset costing $5,184 will be worth exactly $5,184. The existence of the new asset does not affect the accounting for the present $3,000 asset.

Now assume that the cash flows of the $3,000 investment may be broken into components as follows:

TIME	REVENUE	EXPENSES	NET REVENUE
1	10,000	8,220	1,780
2	12,000	10,480	1,520
3	14,400	13,140	1,260

If these numbers are based on a .20 general price level inflation rate, and if there is reason to think that the inflation rate will not be .20, than the forecast of the revenues and expenses should be changed. But they should be changed based on specific information as to how the revenues and expenses will be affected. One cannot assume that all revenues and expenses will change proportionally to changes in the price level. Note that the expenses in the above table did not increase by .20 per year.

Liquidation Value

Because stock prices are expressed in dollars, if the accounting is based on price-level adjusted income measurements, it would be possible to report zero income and still have a situation where the stock price should logically increase.

Assume a situation where an investment fully financed by common stock costs $10,000 and promises to earn $11,000 of cash flows after one year and thus yield .10. If there are 10,000 shares of stock initially outstanding, the stock has value of $1 per share if stockholders are satisfied with a .10 return. The company can be liquidated (shrunk) at any time.

Now assume the price level increases by 100% and the firm earns revenue of $20,000, an amount equal to the price level adjusted depreciation expense. If the $20,000 of revenues are all retained, the firm has cash of $20,000, an amount that will just replace the original equipment. The reported income (with price level adjusted depreciation) will be zero. What should happen to the common stock price? A $20,000 stock value is logical.

Assume there are still 10,000 shares of stock outstanding. The stock initially had a value of $1 per share, but now the company has $20,000 of cash. The stock has a value of $2 per share despite the fact that the zero earnings were reported. The investment of the $20,000 must promise a sufficient return at the end of the next year to justify the investment. The stockholders will have more dollars coming in from the $20,000 investment than they did when the investment was $10,000 (the dollars will, of course, be worth less).

Since the price level doubled over the life of the asset, it is true that the stockholders have not improved their initial position in real terms (this is consistent with zero earnings). In terms of beginning of the year dollars the value of the stock is still $10,000. However, the analyst considering the stock at time 1 will want to know that the stock dollar value should be double the beginning of the year value.

A zero income resulting from price level adjusted depreciation could imply a constant stock price, or even a decline in stock price, to the investor using the price level adjusted earnings. But this conclusion does not follow at all, since the stock price is in dollar terms and the zero income is in real terms. Price level adjusted depreciation may present a bad (confusing and misleading) signal to the investor in common stock.

Leverage: An Alternative Analysis

The amount of debt will now be entered into the analysis not by computing the monetary gains and losses associated with monetary assets and liabilities, but rather by analyzing the residual value to stockholders.

Assume that the following facts apply to two firms, one with zero and one with 40% debt. Except for capital structure the firms are identical:

	Zero Debt	40% Debt
Current earnings before interest	$ 1,000	$ 1,000
Total capital	10,000	10,000
Amount of debt	0	4,000
Interest (10%)	0	400
Earnings to stockholders	1,000	600
Number of shares	1,000	600
Earnings per share	1.00	1.00

Both firms earn $1 per share. Now we will project the results of the next year if we assume a 20% increase in earnings resulting from a 20% inflation. The earnings before interest are expected to increase 20% to $1,200.

	Zero Debt	40% Debt
Earnings before interest	$1,200	$1,200
Interest	0	400
Earnings to stockholders	$1,200	$ 800
Earnings per share	1.20	1.33

The debt flow does not change with the inflation, since it is contractual. During a period of surprise inflation the existence of debt will tend to enhance the position of the stockholders if the income before interest increases. The company with the 40% debt increased earnings per share from $1 to $1.33. The company with zero debt increased earnings from $1 to $1.20. The leverage was beneficial, since the return on investment increased higher than the cost of debt.

If the company had 70% debt outstanding, the new earnings per share would be:

$$\text{EPS} = \frac{1,200 - 700}{300} = \frac{500}{300} = \$1.67$$

If the inflation had been 36% instead of 20% and if earnings before interest had increased proportionately, we would have for the 70% debt firm:

$$\text{EPS} = \frac{1,360 - 700}{300} = \frac{660}{300} = \$2.20$$

versus $1.36 per share with zero debt.

It is possible to do a reasonable analysis of the effects of inflation with a given capital structure without the use of constant dollar accounting. If earnings increase proportional to inflation and if the real cost of debt is negative (as in the above examples), the use of debt will be desirable.

Conclusions

Conventional accounting may give better financial information than price level adjustment information if the inflation expectations are captured in the original purchase decision. The price level adjustment under these conditions introduces distortions into the measures of assets and stock equity. If the inflation was expected, then there is no reason to expect that the price level adjustments will be an improvement over conventional accounting.

If the inflation is a surprise, then the price level adjustments are apt to be beneficial. An empirical study by Baran, Lakonishok, and Ofer (1) appears to support the hypothesis that price level adjusted data contain information not presented using conventional data. This would be related to the fact that the magnitude of the inflation was not expected for the period that was studied.

The accounting profession is apt to recommend changes in accounting that will translate into real terms the depreciation expenses and possibly some other items. The analyst of common stock will have to be careful of these data, since the income measures presented may be misleading. Zero price level adjusted incomes may not be an indication that the stock price should not be increasing. It must be remembered the stock prices are expressed in dollars that are not price level adjusted.

The investor should distinguish between situations where additional investment, if made, will be made based on economic analysis, and where additional capacity will be built because the industry has to react to demand (e.g., public utilities) or where the management of the industry reacts emotionally rather than as a result of economic analysis aimed at maximizing profit.

The analysis of this chapter has been made from the point of view of common stock valuation. If another use of the accounting data is being contemplated, then further analysis of the relative merits of conventional and price level adjusted accounting would be necessary. The relative usefulness of any accounting method will depend on the use to which it is being put.

References

1. BARAN, A., LAKONISHOK, J., and OFER, A. R., "The Information of General Price Level Adjusted Earnings: Some Empirical Evidence," *The Accounting Review,* January 1980, pp. 22–35.

2. BIERMAN, H., JR., "Discounted Cash Flows, Price Level Adjustments and Expectations," *The Accounting Review,* October 1971, pp. 693–699.

3. DAVIDSON, S., SKELTON, L. B., and WEIL, R. L., "Financial Report- and Changing Prices," *Financial Analysts Journal,* May-June 1979, pp. 41–54.

4. FASB, *Statement of Financial Accounting Standards No. 33,* "Financial Reporting and Changing Prices" (Stamford, Conn.: FASB, 1979).

5. MODIGLIANI, F., and COHN, R. A., "Inflation and the Stock Market," *Financial Analysts Journal,* March-April 1979, pp. 24–44.

Key Ideas to Remember

1. The price level adjusted income statement might not give reliable indicators as to whether the common stock price should go up or down.

2. Conventional accounting supplies useful information for common stock valuation, but adjustment may be desirable. With monetary assets price level adjustments are less necessary for stock valuation.

3. Stock prices are expressed in dollars. Real value changes can be misleading for stock valuation.

4. Price level accounting will not replace careful analysis in determining the value of common stock.

5. A constant dollar income statement is likely to be least useful for stock valuation purposes when the assets are of a monetary nature.

6. With surprise inflation, real assets require price level adjustment for the accounting reports to be useful.

7. The value of common stock is equal to the risk adjusted present value of the cash flows from the firm to the stockholders. Price level adjustments to the accounting statements might not help in making these estimates.

SEVEN

Capital Budgeting and Inflation

With prices now so very high
And every purchase drastic,
No one has strength to carry cash—
We pay by check or plastic.

FMK

Inflation is frustrating to corporate managers. They feel strongly that they "should do something." Inflation is beyond their immediate control, but a wide range of decisions affected by inflation are within their control. Unfortunately the adjustments made for inflation in practice frequently are of an incorrect nature. Corporations too often mix and match the several possible adjustments and end up with calculations that are extremely misleading. We will consider to what extent the investment decision process of a corporation (using present value or the internal rate of return methods of evaluating investments) should be affected by forecasts of inflation.

The Problem

If there is rapid inflation, we know that prices will change dramatically in the future and intuitively we suspect that an adjustment in the investment process should be made. We need to define four terms:

Nominal dollars: revenue and costs are measured as they will be measured when the cash is received and disbursed.

Constant dollars: revenue and costs in nominal dollars are adjusted to reflect changes in purchasing power.

Nominal interest rates: the actual cost of money computed using nominal dollars.

Real interest rate: the cost of money if there were market equilibrium and no inflation.

Combining the wrong dollars with the wrong interest rate gives rise to the major errors in capital budgeting under inflationary conditions.

Assume the one-period inflation rate is .12, and that one-period debt costs .15 and the following investment is available with an internal rate of return of .18. These dollar measures are nominal dollars.

0	1	IRR
−1,000	+1,180	.18

The investment is acceptable. If $1,000 of capital is obtained at time zero, then $1,150 must be paid at time 1. There will be $30 of net gain at time 1, over and above the capital costs. Nominal dollars and the nominal cost of obtaining capital can be used to evaluate an investment.

If we use constant dollars (price level adjusted dollars), we have $(1,180/1.12 = 1,054)$:

0	1	real return
−1,000	+1,054	.054

Is the investment yielding a .054 real return acceptable? Would it be acceptable if the inflation rate were .18? The investment is still acceptable as long as the borrowing rate remains at .15. We cannot use the real return of .054 and the actual borrowing rate of .15 to evaluate the investment. The real return of

.054 must be compared to the real cost of borrowing funds, not the nominal return.

Measuring Cash Flows

There are several ways of incorporating inflation forecasts into cash flow forecasts. The most straightforward method is to forecast the rate of inflation and the effect the price level change will have on the cash flows. If a 10% increase in the price level will cause a 10% increase in cash flows, and if the cash flow of period 1 is $100, we would forecast $110 for period 2 if there are no other changes. Instead of a 10% inflation causing a 10% increase in the cash flows, we could have the 10% inflation cause an x% increase in the cash flows of the firm where x is determined by detailed economic analysis relative to the specific situation that the firm is facing.

Rather than use the forecast of the actual dollars to be received (nominal dollars), some analysts prefer to deflate the forecast dollars into dollars of common or real purchasing power (or constant dollars).

For example, if $220 is to be received at time 1 when the price level has increased by 10%, the $220 forecast would be divided by 1.10 and changed into $200 of today's purchasing power. The "real" dollars cannot then be discounted by observed market rates of interest, but rather a "real" rate of interest must be estimated and used.

Another technique that is used in practice is to assume no changes in the purchasing power of the monetary unit. This procedure is not to be recommended unless one really believes the price indexes of the future will be the same as the price index of today, or alternatively, the forecast cash flows are independent of the general purchasing power of the dollar.

While there are several ways for a firm to take inflationary expectations into consideration, we shall recommend here the use of expected cash flows and the observed borrowing rate. Risk adjustments would than be added to the analysis. In this formulation the expected cash flows should reflect the forecast of inflation. Each component of cash flows should be adjusted based on reasonable expectations of cash flows that will be affected by the inflation.

For example, assume an investment costs $200 and is expected to have a life of two years. It is expected that there will be a 15% inflation in the general price level. Assume that based on the inflationary forecast the cash flows of period 1 are expected to be $110 and of period 2 to be $121.

This investment has an internal rate of return of 10% based on the expected cash flows. If funds can be borrowed at a cost of less than 10%, the stockholders' position will be improved if the cash flows are certain. If funds are borrowed at a cost of 10%, the firm will just break even. For example, if the funds are borrowed at 10% and the funds generated by the investment are used to repay the loan, the stockholders would exactly break even.

Initial debt	$200
Interest period 1	20
	$220
First payment	110
Debt at time 1	$110
Interest period 2	11
	$121
Second payment	121
Amount owed at time 2	0

To analyze the above investment, it was necessary to make sure that the cash flow forecasts incorporated the effects of the expected level of price changes. It was not necessary to convert the cash flows into dollars of common purchasing power.

In the above example, the cash flows of the investment were certain and the funds used were borrowed; thus it was only necessary to determine whether the rate of return of the investment was larger than the borrowing rate. If the funds used were supplied by the stockholders and the cash flows are not certain, we have not determined whether or not stockholders are better off at the end of the investment period than at the beginning in real terms. We can determine whether or not the firm is better off with or without the investment using the above technique if the required return is defined and if the cash flows are certain. An additional step is required to determine whether or not the stockholders are actually better off at the end of the period than at the beginning.

Changing the Expectations

Assume the following cash flows are projected if the inflation rate is .10. The firm's current three-period borrowing rate is .10.

TIME	
0	− 1,000.00
1	+ 153.94
2	+ 153.94
3	+ 1,153.94

This investment has an internal rate of return of .15394, and if a discount rate of .10 is used as the hurdle rate, the investment is acceptable.

Assume that some members of management think that .20 is the appropriate discount rate and the projected inflation rate is .15. If .20 is used as the discount rate, the net present value of the above set of cash flows is negative.

Should the investment be rejected?

Solution

If .20 is used as the discount rate the cash flow projection should be made to be consistent with a .15 inflation rate.

Assume that with .15 inflation rather than .10 the cash flows are increased as follows:

Period	Nominal Dollars: Cash Flows	PV (.20)	Present Value
0	− 1,000	1.0000	− 1,000
1	160	.8929	143
2	200	.7972	159
3	1,500	.5787	868
			NPV 170

This new set of cash flows (inflation adjusted) is acceptable using .20 as a discount rate.

We conclude that the present value factors implicitly assume given inflation rates. The same assumed inflation rate must be used both for the cash flow estimates and the rate of discount that is used.

The method of analysis for investment decisions is easily described. We advocate the use of the actual cash flows forecast (including inflation forecasts) and the actual costs of money (not the real required return) to obtain a workable method of capital budgeting under inflationary conditions. The cash flows being used should reflect the inflation that is being forecast.

An Example

Assume the following facts apply for an investment being considered by a firm.

Period	Nominal Dollars: Cash Flows	Price Index
0	− 18,017	100
1	10,000	112
2	10,800	125.44

The firm can borrow funds at a cost of .09, and we assume for simplicity that all the capital being used is debt. Using a .09 discount rate, the investment has a net present value of $247 and the investment seems to be acceptable if the cash flows are certain. The conclusion is consistent with the fact that the investment's internal rate of return is .10, which is greater than the cost of money.

Some firms do not use the above analysis. They argue that the stated cash flows are in terms of nominal dollars and these nominal dollar forecasts fail to reflect the change in purchasing power. Converting the nominal cash flows to constant dollars, we obtain the following cash flows:

PERIOD	NOMINAL DOLLARS: CASH FLOWS	PRICE LEVEL ADJUSTMENT	CONSTANT DOLLARS
0	− 18,017	1	− 18,017
1	10,000	100/112	8,929
2	10,800	100/125.44	8,610

Now the net present value of the constant dollars using .09 is a negative $2,579. The analysis indicates the investment is now not acceptable. But it is an error to convert nominal dollars to constant dollars and use the nominal interest rate of .09.

In this situation, the easy straightforward solution is the correct solution. One can use the nominal dollar cash flows and the nominal interest rates and arrive at a decision that is consistent with maximizing the well-being of the stockholders. For example, if $18,017 is borrowed at a cost of .09, we would have:

TIME	AMOUNT OWED	CASH ALOW OF INVESTMENT: AMOUNT PAID TO DEBT HOLDERS
0	18,017	
1	19,639	10,000
2	10,506	10,506 + 294 amount left over (the inflow is $10,800)

After using the investment's cash flows to pay the debt, there is $294 leftover for the residual investors.

The nominal dollar cash flows show a .08 increase in the benefits of period 2 compared to the benefits of period 1. This might reflect price changes as well as other considerations.

We reach two conclusions:

1. The use of nominal dollars and nominal interest rates is a correct procedure.

2. The use of constant dollars and nominal interest rates is an erroneous procedure.

The use of constant dollars and nominal interest rates is an erroneous procedure in the sense that it can indicate an investment should be rejected even though stockholders benefit from undertaking the investment.

It can be argued that an investment should be rejected since the investors will be worse off at the end of the period than at the beginning of the period. This is the wrong comparison. We should determine if the investors are better off with the investment than without it. For example, now assume that the investors start with $18,017 of capital at time zero and they can lend funds external to the firm and earn .09. The .09 is accepted as a reasonable measure of the opportunity cost of funds. If the above investment is undertaken, after two periods the investor will have:

Terminal value = 10,000 (1.09) + 10,800 = $21,700

but adjusted for inflation this amount will only be worth in terms of beginning of period purchasing power:

$$\frac{21,700}{1.2544} = \$17,299$$

The position of the investor at time 2 with the investment is worse than it was at time zero. However, this is the wrong comparison if the decision is to accept or reject the investment. Let us consider how the investor would have done without the investment. The amount of dollars at time 2 would be:

$$18,017 \ (1.09)^2 = \$21,406$$

and price level adjusted this is:

$$\frac{21,406}{1.2544} = \$17,065$$

The investor is better off with the investment than without it. The fact that the financial position of the investor has deteriorated is not relevant for deciding whether or not to undertake the investment. If .09 truly represents the return from the best alternatives, then the investment is acceptable if it earns at least .09.

Example

Assume an investment would have the following nominal dollar cash flows with an internal rate of return of .10 if the forecast is zero price change. The nominal cost of new capital is .12. The "real" interest is estimated to be .03.

Time	Cash Flow
0	$-3,000$
1	1,300
2	1,200
3	1,100

But now assume a *general* price level increase of .15 per year is forecast for the next three years so that if the cash flows of the investment increased by the same amount, we would have:

Time	Cash Flow	Price Level Adjustment	Nominal Dollars (Adjusted Cash Flow)
0	$-3,000$	$(1.15)^0$	$-3,000$
1	1,300	$(1.15)^1$	1,495
2	1,200	$(1.15)^2$	1,587
3	1,100	$(1.15)^3$	1,673

The above adjusted cash flows would be used to evaluate the investment unless management were willing to forecast the *specific* effects of inflation on the prices and costs of its products. If the adjusted cash flows were used, a discount rate of .12, not the real rate of .03, would be appropriate.

It should be noted that the .12 is not an equilibrium rate of interest. If the inflation rate is .15 and if investors want a real return of .03, then it is necessary for the investment to return:

$$k = .15 + .03 + (.03)(.15) = .1845$$

For example, with a one-period investment of $10,000, one would have to receive $11,845. The $11,845 converts to $11,845/1.15 = $10,300 of price level deflated dollars. The $10,300 leads to a .03 real return on the $10,000 initial investment.

The Use of Constant Dollars

In the above examples constant dollars were used incorrectly. In some situations the investor prefers not to forecast the cash flows in nominal dollars but is able and willing to forecast the constant dollar cash flows. The use of constant dollars bypasses the necessity of forecasting the inflation rate (it can be argued that the bypassing is only approximate since assumptions are being implicitly made). If the cash flows are in constant dollars, the real interest rate should be used, not the nominal (observed) rate. Unfortunately, while the nominal borrowing rate can be observed in the capital makets, the real interest rate cannot be so observed. It must be estimated, and there is no consensus as to its equilibrium value. However, a real opportunity cost of money can be estimated. In equilibrium, we can hypothesize that:

Normal rate = real rate + inflation rate
+ the product of the two

Thus if the real rate were .04 and the inflation rate were .12, we would expect the nominal rate to be:

Normal rate $= .04 + .12 + (.04)(.12) = .1648$

Assume \$100 is invested to earn .1648. After one year the investor will have \$116.48. But \$116.48 converted to constant dollars with an inflation rate of .12 is $\$116.48 / 1.12 = \$104$. Thus the investor earned a real return of .04 on the initial investment of \$100.

If there is not equilibrium in the capital market, the above mathematical relationship can be used to estimate the real interest rate that is effective. We can observe the nominal interest rate and the actual inflation rate and can compute the real return that can actually be earned. The return would be a real opportunity cost. For example, assume investors can earn .1424 by investing in government securities when there is .12 inflation per year. This implies that investors can earn a real return (r) of .02:

$$.1424 = r + .12 + .12r$$

$$(1 + .12)r = .0224$$

$$r = .02$$

The .02 can be used as a real discount rate, since it represents the real opportunity cost for the investor.

A Capacity Problem

A firm with a cost of money of .10 can build a large plant with excess capacity or a small plant and than expand at time 3. The relevant cash flows with zero inflation are:

	0	1	2	3
Large plant	$-20{,}000$			
Small plant	$-10{,}000$			$-13{,}310$

With the above facts the firm is indifferent, since the present value of both sets of outlays using .10 is \$20,000.

Now assume that the general price level is expected to increase at .10, and construction costs at .16 per year. Three-year money costs the firm .15.

What should the firm do? (Assume zero taxes.)

The plant at time 3 will cost:

$$13,310 \ (1.16)^3 = \$20,776$$

Using .15 as the discount rate, we have a present value of:

$$20,776 \ (1.15)^{-3} = \$13,661$$

The additional capacity purchased now only costs $10,000. The larger plant should be built now. A change in the cost of money or rate of price inflation could change the conclusion.

Investments: Timing

The timing of investments will be determined by the cost of borrowing funds and the expected rate of inflation. The relevant inflation rate in this situation is the price index of the cost of the asset to be acquired. We will assume technology change is not a factor.

For simplicity assume a zero tax rate. Funds can be borrowed at a cost of .10. An asset would cost $1,000,000 if constructed now, and the cost is expected to increase at a rate of .20 per year. The firm knows it wants the asset, the only decision is as to timing. With the facts as described the asset should be acquired as soon as feasible. If $1,000,000 is borrowed, after one year the firm will have the asset and will owe $1,100,000. If the firm waits one year, it will have the asset and will owe $1,200,000 because of the .20 increase in cost.

If the facts are changed so that the inflation rate is only .06 and if the acquisition can be delayed, it should be delayed. With delay at time 1 the firm will only have to pay $1,060,000 compared to $1,100,000 if it is acquired now at a cost of $1,000,000. This assumes no change in other cash flows.

If we remove the assumption of a zero tax rate, the analysis is more complex since the tax basis of the asset changes. Assume the tax rate is .46. The cost of debt must be placed after tax and the change in tax basis must be considered. Assume the present value of the tax savings is equal to $.40 per dollar of cost. The cost of debt is .10 before tax and .054 after tax. Assume there is .20 inflation in cost:

	0	*1*
Buy now	− 1,000,000	
Borrow	+ 1,000,000	− 1,054,000
PV of tax savings	+ 400,000	
Invest (.054)	− 400,000	+ 421,600
Total	0	− 632,400
Buy at time 1		− 1,200,000
PV of tax savings		+ 480,000
Total		− 720,000

Assume the $400,000 is invested to earn .054 after tax.

Buying now is more desirable than waiting one year. An outlay of $632,400 at time 1 is better than an outlay of $720,000 at time 1.

As long as one is willing to use the after tax borrowing rate to compute present values, we can reach a generalization. If the inflation rate is greater than the after tax borrowing rate, it will be costly to the firm to delay the acquisition. In fact, delay is desirable only if the after tax discount factor is greater than the rate of inflation.

Capacity, Profit Potential, and Inflation*

Inflation implies a shifting demand curve for a firm's products. If a price of $10 per unit will result in 20 units being demanded to-

---

* This section is based on a paper written by the author titled "Capacity Measures and Financial Accounting," published in *Accounting and Business Research,* Autumn 1975.

day, with inflation the same 20 units are likely to be sold for a higher price. If the price is kept at $10, then it is likely that more than 20 units will be demanded.

We want to consider this latter situation in more detail. The objective is to determine to what extent the capacity of the industry and the capacity of the specific firm affect the ability of a firm to benefit from an inflationary situation.

A comparison of the actual level of operations and the economic capacity of a company is an element in determining the profit prospects of a firm. Unless the reader of a financial report has this information, it is impossible to estimate the opportunity for expansion for unit sales without additional investment. In addition to the information about the capacity utilization of the company, information about the capacity utilization of the industry is also of interest. It tells us something about the nature of the price competition the firm faces.

While the definition of capacity is difficult for multiproduct firms, an attempt should be made to supply this information by product line. A comparison of the actual activity and the economic capacity is relevant information to the financial analyst and should be supplied along with the other financial information.

The Relevance of Capacity

Figure 1 illustrates the relevance of an industry's percentage of capacity. Assume an industry is operating as shown in Figure 1. The output is Q_0 and the price is P_0. The kink in the supply curve arises from the assumption that if the industry is to supply more than Q_c units, it will have to build more plant and equipment. The long-run marginal cost (LRMC) curve reflects these fixed costs not yet incurred. We define Q_c, the point where the short-run marginal cost (SRMC) and the long-run marginal cost (LRMC) curves intersect, to be capacity of the industry (or firm). If more

Figure 1   Capacity of an Industry

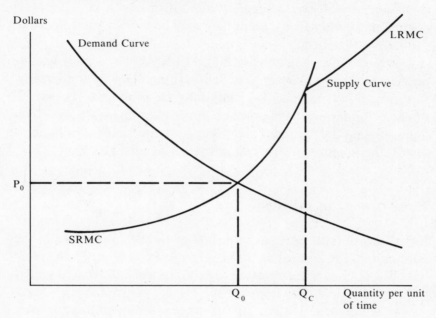

units than Q_C are demanded, more productive facilities will be built.

In Figure 1, Q_C the intersection of SRMC, the short-run marginal cost curve, and LRMC, the long-run marginal cost curve, is the industry capacity. The two curves differ in that LRMC includes the capital costs (interest and depreciation costs of new plant and equipment) that are excluded from the SRMC curve. Both curves will change after the productive capacity has been expanded and the costs of the new plant and equipment become sunk (not relevant) costs.

If the industry has a great deal of excess capacity, we can expect the SRMC curve to be relatively flat. A shift in the demand curve to the right would then result in a large increase in output but only a slight increase in price. As drawn in Figure 1 the SRMC curve increases rapidly, and a shift to the right in demand will result in a large increase in price that draws forth an increase in physical output when output exceeds Q_C. If the industry has a small amount of excess capacity but a firm has a large amount compared to other firms, then there may be the potential for large profits for that firm.

In some situations the SRMC and LRMC curves may not intersect, but rather there is a discontinuity. Using the present facilities, no more than Q_C units may be produced because of physical limitations. To produce more than Q_C units again requires capital outlays, and a sufficiently large increase in price to justify the investment. This situation is illustrated in Figure 2.

The Relevance of Inflation

Inflation will tend to result in a shift of the demand curve to the right and a shift upward of the supply curve of Figure 1. The same quantity of units will cost more to produce and will sell at a higher price.

Whether or not inflation encourages the investment in new plant and equipment will depend on the relative shifts in the demand curve and the SRMC and the LRMC curves.

For example, assume a situation where the demand curve shifts to the right. The short-run marginal cost portion of the supply curve (the costs) does not change.

Whether or not the increased price will draw forth investment in new capacity will depend on how much the long-run marginal cost curve has shifted upward compared to the shift in the demand curve. The slope (rate of increase) in the short-run marginal cost curve will also affect the decision to invest, since the increased demand might be satisfied by using the current assets more intensively.

In some situations an industry might have a well-defined output limitation that it cannot exceed without additional investment. That limit is Q_C in Figure 2. With the situation shown in Figure 2, if no new facilites were forthcoming, a shift in the demand curve to the right would first result in increased output to Q_C and then

Figure 2

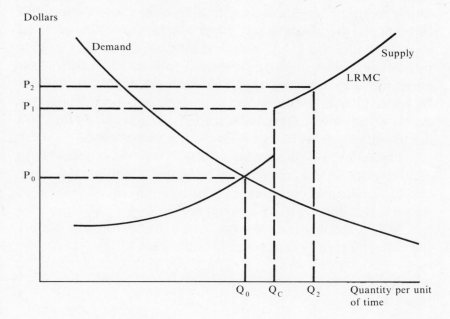

Dollars

would merely result in increased prices, since Q_C is the maximum number of units that can be produced without additional capital investments. Only if the price were to increase as high as P_1 would the industry have economic incentive to add to its productive capacity.

The industry capacity situation affects the profit potential of a firm with excess capacity. Assume the situation of Figure 2 applies and that the demand shifts so that the price goes to P_2 and output to Q_2. The firm that could expand production (supplying, say $Q_C - Q_0$ units) would reap windfall profits. In a situation where an industry had $Q_C - Q_0$ of excess capacity, it would be useful investment information to know which individual firms possessed that excess capacity. The amount of industry excess capacity is also relevant, since unused capacity tends to limit price increases.

One rule to follow in investing during inflationary periods

when demand curves are shifting to the right is to seek out an industry requiring large amounts of fixed assets, where additional investments are discretionary, and where the entire physical capacity is likely to be utilized; in this situation the price is likely to increase. The second step is to find firms in the industry that currently have excess capacity. This strategy implies that one can forecast shifts in industry demand curves and can identify the degree of capacity utilization by the firm. If you can do this, you are identifying firms likely to benefit from inflation.

Figure 3 shows the profits of a firm with excess capacity (a relatively flat SRMC curve) before and after a shift in the demand curve (represented by the marginal revenue curves). It is assumed that the firm faces sloping demand curves.

MR_0 is the marginal revenue of the firm before and MR_1 is the marginal revenue after the shift in demand. The incremental

Figure 3

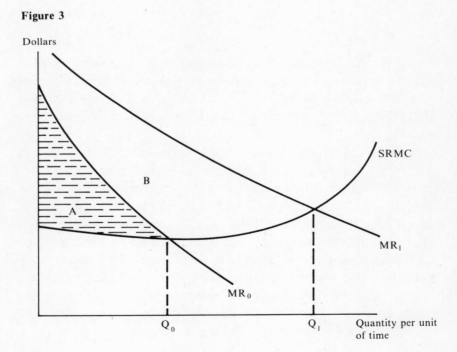

profits of the firm before the demand shift are the hatched area labeled A, and after the demand shift the profits are A plus the area labeled B. The firm profits from the fact that the shift in demand enables it to sell $(Q_1 - Q_0)$ more units and to sell all the units (Q_1) at a higher price (the price is not shown). The presence of excess capacity effectively means that the firm can expand output with only a slight rise in SRMC.

The price necessary to attract investment to the industry is likely to be much higher than the price necessary to draw forth more production when there is excess capacity (the portion of the SRMC curve that is relatively flat). This arises since the SRMC curve excludes the costs of the fixed factors of production (plant and equipment) but the LRMC curve includes these costs.

It is interesting that the high prices used in the investment analysis are apt to be excessively optimistic. Once the productive capacity has been expanded the LRMC is no longer relevant since there is a new SRMC curve based on the available resources. This new SRMC curve is then price and output influencing. Thus the price of P_1 shown in Figure 2 may be a temporary price that will be brought down as soon as the new capacity comes on line.

Table 7-1 shows a possible interaction on profit potential between industry capacity being used and the percentage of capacity of the firm being used.

If the industry is using a low percentage of capacity (high excess capacity) then the outlook of the firm is not good, especially

TABLE 7-1. Profit Growth Potential

		Industry: percentage of capacity being used	
Firm:		<u>low</u>	<u>high</u>
percentage of	<u>low</u>	modest	very high
capacity being used	<u>high</u>	very low	modest

if the firm is producing at near capacity (it will not be able to expand output profitably, since the industry has excess capacity). If the industry is operating at high percentage of capacity but the firm has a large amount of excess capacity, the profit potential is very large. The firm can expand with no additional plant investment, but its competitors do not have the capacity for expanding. If the company and the industry are both operating close to capacity, then the opportunity for "easy profit" does not exist, but at least all the firms are in more or less the same position. To produce more, there will have to be more investment in plant and equipment. With this situation we know that if the firm is operating at capacity, further profits are going to come from higher prices, efficiencies, or additional investment. If the firm is operating at less than capacity, then additional profits may be earned as well by increasing output without making additional investment in plant and equipment.

Conclusions

We have illustrated a correct and an incorrect method of evaluating investments under conditions of inflation. We have not attempted to illustrate all the possible combinations of incorrect calculations. The discounted cash flow calculations are powerful tools of analysis, but if the inputs do not have a sound theoretical foundation, the output is not useful.

   If is reasonable to want to adjust for inflation. The calculation of cash flows using nominal dollars does adjust for inflation in the sense that the nominal dollar forecast reflects the expected price changes. While the adjustment to constant dollars is useful in evaluating whether the investor is better or worse off at the end of the period than at the beginning, it is difficult to use constant dollars to make accept or reject investment decisions. The combinations of constant dollars and the nominal interest rates is a major error.

Key Ideas to Remember

1. In making investment decisions, nominal dollars should only be used with nominal interest rates.

2. In making investment decisions, constant dollars should only be used with real interest rates.

3. An investment might leave an investor worse off at the end of the period than at the beginning and still be desirable.

4. If the inflation rate is greater than the after tax borrowing rate, it is costly to delay the acquisition of an asset.

5. No adjustments for price level changes are better than bad adjustments.

6. The amount of excess capacity in an industry and amount of excess capacity of a firm are very relevant bits of information for financial analysis.

7. Using the forecast cash flows is a safe, theoretically correct way of making capital budgeting decisions.

EIGHT

Measuring Performance and Inflation

When we see our yearly income
We feel rich as Croesus
Then we view the new expenses
And our dreams collapse in pieces.
It really seems ironic that
Since our income soared
There's less and less in real goods
The firm can still afford.

FMK

The present rate of increase in the general price level is too large and persistent for managers operating in many different countries to ignore. Unfortunately, in their attempt to use more sophisticated measures, managers are frequently introducing new errors into their analysis.

This chapter will consider performance measurement under conditions of inflation. Initially we will make the simplifying assumption that monetary gains equal monetary losses (as when the firm has no net monetary assets and all financing is done with common stock). The objective of the chapter is to illustrate the type of situation where price level adjusted accounting leads to reasonable measures of performance and where the results can be misleading. Finally, the financial information resulting from the application of FAS 33 is evaluated.

An Equilibrium Situation: Surprise Inflation

Assume a situation where an investment costs $3,000 and promises to earn the following cash flows with a zero inflation rate:

PERIOD	CASH FLOW
1	1,455
2	1,157
3	902

The internal rate of return of this investment is .0909. Using the present value method of depreciation (depreciation expense is the change in value of the asset), the measures shown in Table 8–1 result.

The return on investment (ROI) is a constant .09 each time period and is equal to the internal rate of return. Now assume there is a surprise: .10 inflation each year and the cash flows, incomes and ROIs shown in Table 8–2 occur. We will initially use the same amount of depreciation expense in each year as is used in Table 8–1.

The management can properly observe that inflation was a major factor leading to the improved returns compared to the projected returns. Assume the firm adjusts both depreciation expense and net investment for the .10 inflation per year. The adjustments are as in Table 8–3.

TABLE 8–1. Return on Investment

PERIOD	CASH FLOW	PRESENT VALUE AT BEGINNING OF PERIOD (.0909)	CHANGE IN VALUE: DEPRECIATION	INCOME	ROI
1	1,455	3,000	1,181	274	.09
2	1,157	1,819	992	165	.09
3	902	827	827	75	.09

TABLE 8-2. Inflation of .10 per Year

Period	Cash Flows	Depreciation	Income	Investment	ROI
1	1,600	1,181	419	3,000	.14
2	1,400	992	408	1,819	.22
3	1,200	827	373	827	.45

TABLE 8-3. Price Level Adjustments

Period	Depreciation		Price Level Depreciation	Investment		Price Level Investment
1	1,181 × 1.1	=	1,299	3,000 × 1.1	=	3,300
2	992 × 1.21	=	1,201	1,819 × 1.21	=	2,201
3	827 × 1.331	=	1,101	827 × 1.331	=	1,101

Using these price level adjusted measures, we again earn a .09 return on investments each year, but now this is a real return if the price index effectively measures the change in purchasing power (see Table 8-4).

In the above special example, as long as management realizes that the ROI being measured is a real and not a nominal measure, the procedure is effective. In the example, the management earned a real return of .09. This is equal to the return that would have been earned with zero inflation and if the original forecast cash flows had been earned.

TABLE 8-4. Price Level Adjusted Information

Period	Cash Flow	Price Level Depreciation	Income	Price Level Investment	ROI
1	1,600	1,299	301	3,300	.09
2	1,400	1,201	199	2,201	.09
3	1,200	1,101	99	1,101	.09

Let us define:

k   as the investment's internal rate of return using cash flows

r   as the investment's real rate of return

j   as the inflation rate

Then if:

$$k = r + j + rj$$

the real return of r will be earned. An alternative interpretation is that if the investor wants a real return r with an inflation rate of j, a cash flow rate of return of k must be earned.

In this example the final internal rate of return of the investment is .20. This is exactly equal to:

$$k = r + j + rj$$

if a real return of .0909 is required and the inflation rate is .10:

$$k = .0909 + .10 + .0091 = .20$$

If funds can be obtained at a nominal cost of .20, the investment being studied will exactly break even, and we can speak of this as being an equilibrium situation. The capital earning .20 will return the required real return of .0909 if there is .10 inflation.

In the above example the first set of cash flows was forecast assuming a zero inflation rate. Now let us assume that the investment still costs $3,000 and the manager perfectly anticipates the inflation and correctly forecasts the results shown in Table 8–5.

TABLE 8–5.   Return on Investment

PERIOD	CASH FLOWS	DEPRECIATION	INCOME	INVESTMENT	ROI
1	1,600	1,000	600	3,000	.20
2	1,400	1,000	400	2,000	.20
3	1,200	1,000	200	1,000	.20

TABLE 8–6. Price Level Adjusted ROI

Period	Cash Flow	Price Level Depreciation	Income	Price Level Investment	ROI
1	1,600	1,100	500	3,300	.152
2	1,400	1,210	190	2,420	.079
3	1,200	1,331	-131	1,331	negative

As long as the cost of money is equal to or less than .20, this is an acceptable investment. If the market lacks the foresight of our manager, and capital is obtained as a cost lower than .20, then the investment will be undertaken at a cost of $3,000.

Now we will again apply the price level adjustments that were previously applied, but now the inflation has been perfectly forecast. If the same method of depreciation (see Table 8–1) were used, we would again obtain the results of Table 8–4 (a constant ROI of .09). If we assume straight line depreciation unadjusted for inflation (as in Table 8–5), then the results of Table 8–6 occur if the depreciation expenses and investment balances are adjusted for the actual price level changes.

Assume that the required internal rate at the time of the investment was .15. The investment's expected return of .20 was sufficient to justify undertaking it, and the expectations were actually realized. However, the price level adjusted measures of Table 8–6 seem to indicate that the investment was not satisfactory. This is misleading in the sense that the actual monetary return was more than satisfactory. The required return was a monetary return and is not a suitable benchmark to which the price level adjusted ROI can be compared.

Monetary Gains and Losses

The Statement of Financial Accounting Standards No. 33, "Financial Reporting and Changing Prices," requires that major companies disclose the effects of changing prices as supplementary information in their published annual reports. Since top managers of corporations generally want to know how a decision will affect the financial statements of a firm, we can expect that pro forma financial statements will be prepared for proposed investments. In addition we expect that measures of performance will be prepared on a basis to be consistent with the type of price level accounting recommended by FAS 33.

Let us consider Schedule C of FAS 33 (p. 34). The schedule contains two earnings per share measures; one is based on historical cost information, and the second is the "Income (loss) from continuing operations per common share" using adjusted cost information. This latter measure excludes the holding gains and losses ("Gain from decline in purchasing power of net amounts owed"). This exclusion means that the price level adjusted earnings per share measure presented is an incomplete measure with great potential for introducing distortion into the decision processes of corporations, as well as the evaluation of financial affairs. While we will focus on Schedule C, it should be realized that even a theoretically correct price level accounting procedure using a general price index could not be used with great reliability to evaluate investments.

We shall use a simplified example to illustrate the problems introduced into decision making by FAS 33. The only crucial assumption made is that the top decision makers and persons measuring performance adjust for the changes in the price level consistent with the recommendations of FAS 33.

An Example

Assume a plant costing $1,000 is financed entirely with debt costing .10. The plant has a life of 20 years and earns $150 in the first year. The two income statements (conventional and price level adjusted) assuming a doubling of the price levels are:

	Conventional	Price Level Adjusted
Revenues	150	150
Depreciation	50	100
Interest	100	100
Operating income	0	-50
Monetary gain		1,000

The reader of the financial statements has three choices (there are actually more, but this example and set of choices offer enough complexity). Conventional accounting indicates a break-even result while the price level adjusted measure shows a loss of $50. The third alternative is to include the $1,000 monetary gain and show a net income of $950. This latter interpretation is not encouraged by FAS 33. Let us consider the conventional and the price level adjusted balance sheets.

	Conventional Beginning	End	Price Level Adjusted Beginning	End
Cash	0	50	0	50
Plant	1,000	950	2,000	1,900
Debt	1,000	1,000	2,000	1,000
Stock equity	0	0	0	950

The price level adjusted comparative balance sheets show that the firm is better off at the end of the period (stock equity of $950) than at the beginning (stock equity of zero). This is consistent with the net income computed including the monetary gain from being in debt. But following FAS 33 this measure of income is not apt to be used to measure performance. The loss of $50 is more apt to receive attention than the income measure that includes the monetary gain. It is difficult to see how the $50 loss measure can be used for any managerial purpose. It excludes too many factors from consideration (all monetary gains and losses) but at the same time includes a price level effect on the depreciation expense that may not be correct.

A Quick and Dirty Adjustment

Price level adjustments can obviously become very complex and difficult to interpret. Should monetary gains and losses be included? If they are included (or excluded), how should the results be interpreted?

We will consider a relatively simple alternative. Assume a person's income after tax is $10,000 in year 1 and $12,100 in year 2. The price index is 100 in year 1 and 110 in year 2. We want to adjust the incomes to dollars of equal purchasing power. Assume it is decided to adjust year 2's income to year 1's purchasing power. We now have:

$$
\begin{array}{lll}
\text{Year 1} & \$10,000 & \text{of income} \\
\text{Year 2} & \dfrac{\$12,100}{1.10} = & \begin{array}{l}\$11,000 \text{ of income} \\ \text{(in year 1 purchasing power)}\end{array}
\end{array}
$$

There is a real increase in income of $1,000 in terms of year 2 purchasing power. If we adjusted to year 2 purchasing power, the income of year 1 would be $11,000 and the increase in income would be $12,100 − 11,000 = $1,100.

Assume the price index reasonably reflects the person's purchasing power, then the above adjustment does an excellent job of adjusting for inflation. But there are several major omissions from the analysis that we should consider.

What happens to the analysis if there are revenues and expenses and one of the expenses is cost of goods sold and another is depreciation expense? The fact that the costs giving rise to these expenses were incurred in periods of lower prices causes discrepancy between the historical cost measure and the current cost equivalent for the factors of production being used.

A second omission is the fact that the suggested adjustment omits the losses arising from holding monetary assets and the gains from being in debt in a period of inflation.

These omissions should be noted, since they limit the usefulness of the suggested adjustment. The adjustment is a rough adjustment that is decreased in usefulness by the presence of large amounts of real assets being depreciated or a large difference between monetary assets and liabilities.

Conclusions

While we can define conditions under which price level adjusted accounting can lead to performance measures that are useful, it is difficult to do so. There are situations where management has anticipated inflation, and the price level adjustments may actually distort the performance measures. This was illustrated in an example where an investment with a .20 internal rate of return in terms of cash flow and less than a .20 return was required. But the investment earned less than the required return in each year as a result of the price level adjustment.

A second difficulty arises when the monetary gains and losses from inflation are omitted from the income measure. This omission can lead to a distortion in decision making by leading to measures of performance that indicate the investment is not acceptable, even though the financial health of the corporation will be improved by undertaking the investment.

Inflation does introduce additional complexity into the evaluation of investments and the measurement of performance. Using false price level adjustments or correct adjustments that do not apply to a specific situation will not lead to improved managerial performance. Mechanical application of price level adjustments without considering the circumstances will not necessarily result in improved performance measures.

Key Ideas to Remember

1. To earn a real return of r with an inflation rate j, one must earn $r + j + rj$.

2. With perfectly predicted inflation, price level adjusted assets will be overstated.

3. Excluding monetary gains will bias against accepting good investments.

4. For some purposes, not adjusting revenues and expenses, but converting the incomes of different time periods to the same purchasing power might be of use. However, the limitations of this calculation should be noted.

5. In measuring performance, it makes a significant difference whether the inflation was expected or unexpected. Price level adjustments to depreciation expense, if the inflation was expected, can distort more than correct

6. No price level adjustment of plant or other real assets using a price index is going to lead to reliable value or income measures. For many purposes value estimators would be more useful.

NINE

Indexing for Inflation

Governmental profit from inflation,
I fear,
Makes their effort to contain it rather
Insincere.

FMK

This chapter will first analyze a situation where monetary assets (securities) and liabilities are indexed for changes in the price level so that real values stay constant. We will consider a variety of situations so that the consequences of indexing may be better understood. The consequences to firms and to the economy will be investigated. Finally the indexing of depreciation expense will be considered.

Theoretically in a closed economic system it would be possible to devise an indexing system which exactly balanced out the effect of price level changes so that one could buy protection against losses as a result of price level changes. The dollar measures would change, but everyone who desired to buy protection would be protected, and a change in price level would leave real wealth unchanged. While theoretically possible, it is very unlikely that such a system could be implemented in a manner that would leave everyone's wealth position unchanged by inflation. In the real world some people benefit and others are harmed by price

121

changes, and adjustments made using averages (indexes) are not likely to treat everyone the same.

Let us consider the simplest of all situations where inflation occurs that was not anticipated. All things equal, debtors (organizations in debt) are better off compared to their situation before the inflation, and organizations with monetary claims (creditors) are harmed by the inflation. Just considering balance sheet effects, organizations which have equal monetary assets and monetary liabilities are unaffected by the inflation *if* the value of their real assets changes proportionally to the price level change.

Assume a situation where a firm has the following balance sheet:

| Monetary assets | 8,000 | Monetary liabilities | 8,000 |
| Real assets | 2,000 | Stock equity | 2,000 |

If the real assets change in value proportional to the price index, the firm neither gains or loses as a result of price level changes. It is in a hedged position and has no price level risk. The real value of the stockholders' position will be maintained.

If the monetary–real asset mix or the debt-equity ratio is changed, then the firm will enter a situation where it can gain or lose. For example, if $2,000 of real assets were financed 90% by $1,800 of debt and $200 of common stock, then a doubling of the price level (with the value of the real assets doubling) would result in an 11-fold increase in the value of the stock. The value of the $2,000 of real assets would go to $4,000, the liability remains at $1,800, and the stock equity goes from $200 to $2,200, where the $200 is in terms of beginning of the period purchasing power and the $2,200 is in terms of the end of the period purchasing power.

The strategy to be followed by a firm that wants to speculate on price level changes is clear. It should use more debt if it expects more inflation than the market expects, and it should invest in real assets. If it expects deflation, an opposite strategy would be appropriate.

Interest Rates and Indexing

Indexing is not necessary to protect investors in a situation where there is perfectly predicted inflation and the market adjusts the required interest rate to take into consideration the predicted inflation rate.

Assume it is known that the inflation rate will be .12 for the next 12 months and that the investor wants a real growth (earnings) rate of .04. What nominal rate is required?

Let:

> k be the required nominal rate
> r be the real rate required
> j be the inflation rate

Then it can be shown that:

$$(1)\ k = r(1 + j) + j$$

or:

$$(2)\ k = r + j + rj$$

The required nominal growth rate is equal to the sum of the real required return, the inflation rate, and the product of the two. If $r = .04$ and $j = .12$ we have:

$$(1)\ k = .04(1 + .12) + .12$$
$$= .0448 + .12 = .1648$$

The required nominal rate is .1648. An investment of $100 must earn $16.48 for the investor to earn .04 real. If the investment earns $116.48 at time 1, dividing by 1.12 to deflate for the price level change we obtain $116.48/1.12 = $104 in beginning of the period purchasing power. This is .04 larger than $100; thus in real terms the growth is .04 (at the end of the year we have $104 of beginning of the year purchasing power, having started with $100).

Thus if the investors (lenders) know the inflation rate, they can adjust the rate of interest to be charged so that a satisfactory real return is earned. However, if the price level change expectation is exceeded by the actual rate of inflation, the investor may be unpleasantly surprised. For example, if the actual inflation rate turns out to be .25 rather than .12, then the $116.48 end of period investment will be worth only $116.48/1.25 = $93.18 in terms of beginning of the period dollars and the investor will have suffered a real loss. In this situation (imperfectly predicted price level changes) there is an opportunity for the investing firm to improve its risk position by the use of price level indexing. With a .25 inflation rate the investor would receive $104(1.25) = $130 and would earn a real return of .04.

Assume that the investor in the above example rejected the investment yielding .1648, but accepted in its stead an indexed investment that promised to pay one year hence $104 of beginning of the year purchasing power. If the price level goes up by .12, then the end of the year payment for the indexed investment will be:

$$\$104 \times 1.12 = \$116.48$$

and the investor receives exactly the same as the purchaser of the .1648 yielding security. However, if the inflation rate turns out to be .25, the investor buying the indexed security will receive $104 × 1.25 = $130.

The $130 received at the end of the year has $104 of beginning of the year purchasing power; thus the investor has earned the required .04 real return and a nominal .30 return.

The indexed investment eliminates the price level risk independent of the amount of price level change. The adjustment in interest rate .1648 can only protect the investor against one specific value of the expected inflation, .12 in the above example.

Can the investor lose by buying a price level indexed security? While the investor is protected against inflation, it is possible to lose *compared* to what would have been earned. For example, if there is zero inflation (where .12 had been forecast), the indexed investor receives $104 while the investor buying the straight security receives \$116.48. Of course, the risk exposure (risk of price inflation) of the two investors differed considerably. If the price level goes down, the investor may actually receive less than \$100 but still have a .04 real return.

Also, the index being used is likely to be an average and does not insure that the investing firm will be able to buy its specific market basket of goods.

Thus the indexed security offers protection for the investor against one type of risk, and is apt to be attractive to a wide range of investors who are willing to accept a modest real return in order to achieve this type of protection. Other investors will want to have a well-defined monetary return thus will reject indexed securities in favor of low-risk-of-default conventional securities where the interest rate reflects the expected inflation.

Price Indexing and Risk

A firm borrowing money can expect to find lenders willing to offer funds if a real return can be guaranteed. But unless the firm borrowing the funds and promising to pay a real return can invest funds under identical terms (with perhaps a high basic interest rate to cover transaction costs and profit), the risk of inflation will be transferred to the investing firm by the firm (person) borrowing. Assume investing Firm A lends funds to a Firm B that is borrowing funds where the loans are indexed. Now the investing Firm A seems to be hedged against inflation, but unless B's assets are also indexed, B might not be able to pay its debt.

Investing Firm A has an indexed receivable, but the indexing will be only partially effective if the organization (B) borrowing the funds from it does not have perfectly indexed assets. Assume that the assets being financed by the indexed loan are perfectly correlated with the price index. Now we have the happy situation where Firm B has guaranteed its investors against inflation and at the same time is itself protected since its loan is price indexed.

Now assume that Firm B has an asset the value of which is independent of the price index. While the firm's debt is price indexed, it may happen that an increase in the price index will merely result in a defaulted loan rather than a payment with a constant real value. While the amount payable to A will increase, the ability of the debtor to pay the increased obligation is not increased.

The major point of the above example is that for price indexing to protect individuals and organizations against inflation requires a linkage where each link has an indexed liability and an indexed asset. If one or the other is not indexed, or if the amounts are not equal, then inflation risk remains. Even where there seems to be indexing (as when the firm indexes a loan), there may not be effective indexing if the debtor has an asset which is not perfectly correlated with the price index. It is possible to write a legal contract that is not meaningful from an economic point of view. If the debtor (B) cannot pay A, then despite the legal terminology of the loan contract Firm A is not protected from inflation.

Thus if a firm indexes its receivables, the hedging against price level changes may only be a paper hedging because of the inability of the next debtor to meet the inflated loan obligation.

This analysis implies that indexing may not be an effective mechanism for eliminating price level change risk unless indexing is common throughout the economy. For example, unless depreciation expense taken for taxes is indexed, an industrial firm will have a monetary asset (the tax deduction), and its ability to meet its indexed debt payments will be jeopardized.

Indexing of Depreciation

Probably the primary tax "reform" that heavy industry would choose would be the price level indexing of depreciation expense taken as a deduction in computing taxable income. There is no question that government inspired inflation unfairly erodes the value of depreciation deductions. A firm invests $1,000,000 in purchasing power, and when the tax deduction is taken seven years later, it only shields from taxes $500,000 of purchasing power.

Taken in isolation there is little question that fairness dictates that depreciation expense should be adjusted for price level changes. The complication is that many parties are taxed unfairly when there is inflation. The interest on a .10 savings certificate is taxed as income even though there is .12 inflation and real value of the investment plus interest is less at the end of the year than at the beginning. A person earning $10,000 per year is taxed at .20. The same person earning $20,000 per year after prices have doubled may be taxed at .30. In fact, the doubling of prices might be accompanied by an increase in wages to $15,000 and a tax rate of .30. This too is unfair.

If depreciation expense is to be adjusted for price level changes, the justification will have to be that the government wants to reduce the corporate taxes and to supply increased incentives for investment. The change would be consistent with fairness, but fairness cannot be the primary justification given the other widespread unfairnesses.

An alternative to indexing depreciation (which allows industry a windfall, given that the inflation has taken place; industry would not want indexing if there had been deflation) would be for all the investment to be expensed at the time of acquisition. Such a policy would eliminate all problems of the rate of depreciation, the adjustment of depreciation for inflation, and the nature of the gain on retirement or sale of the asset (all gains would be ordinary income).

Indexing of Bonds

A purchasing power bond would offer many advantages to investors. The bond would pay a real interest rate and would have a maturity amount that was tied to some measure of the general price level.

For example, a $1,000 one-year bond paying .04 real interest

would actually pay $80 interest if the price level doubled, and
$2,000 at maturity. By receiving $2,080, the investor has earned a
real return of .04 on the $1,000 investment.

The catch is that the averge borrower (individual, corporation, or government) cannot guarantee being able to pay a real interest rate of .04. The risk of default is present.

Nevertheless, there is reason to consider the use of purchasing
power bonds. They at least tend to reduce one type of risk for the
investors.

Conclusions

To the extent that indexing is not perfectly executed so that all
parties are protected against the effects of inflation, indexing will
lead to redistributions of wealth. For example, the index used will
be an average and will not apply to specific organizations, so some
will benefit from the specific index being used while others will be
harmed.

Indexing has its usefulness as a device for enabling specific
economic entities to eliminate (or at least to reduce) price level
risk. The reduction in risk may have beneficial effects relative to
the welfare of individuals, but it would harm others. It is difficult
to see why indexing would lead inevitably to either positive or
negative effects on the total production of goods and services. It
will affect distributions of wealth.

At the firm level, indexing would lead to a necessity that
managers not promise more than they can deliver relative to the
payment of their liabilities in constant dollars, if the assets of the
firm are not also price indexed in real terms. When the price level
change is largely caused by a major change in costs (as with the recent energy crisis), it would be likely for the expenses of a firm to
also increase. If liabilities are indexed it is still possible that they
are defaulted because of the firm's financed difficulties caused by
the inflation and the energy crisis.

Key Ideas to Remember

1. Theoretically in a closed economic system one could devise an indexing system where one could buy protection against losses as a result of price level changes. In the real world it is not feasible for everyone to be protected.

2. Indexing implies the use of an average index; thus the adjustment might not apply to a firm's specific market basket of goods.

3. A firm (or other entity) promising to pay price level adjusted wages (or debt) might find that it cannot make any payments.

4. Inflation erodes the value of the depreciation expense tax deduction. But this is only one of many inequities arising from the tax laws and inflation.

5. Immediate expensing of assets would help solve the depreciation expense unfairness situation and supply additional incentives for real investment.

6. Indexing tends to lead to higher prices, which in turn lead to more indexing, which tends to lead to a price spiral.

TEN

Interest Rates
(Term Structure)

A brash, young Comptroller was hired,
But his term of employ soon expired.
He indebeted his firm
With debentures—long term—*
Rates fell which required him fired.

FMK

Changes in the rate of inflation will generally be accompanied by changes in the interest rates. If the market does not expect the current economic situation to remain unchanged in the future, we can expect there to be different interest rates for different time periods.

Let us define r_i as the 1-period forward interest rate for time period i.

Consider the situation depicted in the following diagram:

$$\begin{array}{c} \quad .20 \qquad .15 \qquad .10 \\ \vdash\!\!-\!\!-\!\!-\!\!-\!\!-\!\!-\!\!-\!\!-\!\!-\!\!-\!\!-\!\!-\!\!-\!\!\dashv \\ 0 \quad r_1 \quad 1 \quad r_2 \quad 2 \quad r_3 \quad 3 \end{array}$$

We have for the 1-period forward rates:

$$r_1 = .20$$
$$r_2 = .15$$
$$r_3 = .10$$

* Of course we are assuming a non-callable bond.

The present value factors to discount future cash flows back to time zero using these rates are:

TIME		PRESENT VALUE FACTORS
1	1.20^{-1} =	.8333
2	$1.20^{-1} \times 1.15^{-1}$ =	.7246
3	$1.20^{-1} \times 1.15^{-1} \times 1.10^{-1}$ =	.6588

The value of r_1 may be observed directly, but the values of r_2 and r_3 must be derived from the yields of one-, two-, and three-period securities.

We also find it useful to define a yield to maturity of R_i. R_i is a special type of average of the forward rates. Thus for one period we have:

$$(1 + R_1) = 1 + r_1$$
$$R_1 = .20$$

For a cash flow at time 2:

$$(1 + R_2)^2 = (1 + r_1)(1 + r_2)$$
$$(1 + R_2)^2 = (1.20)(1.15) = 1.38$$
$$1 + R_2 = 1.1747$$
$$R_2 = .1747$$

For a cash flow at time 3:

$$(1 + R_3)^3 = (1 + r_1)(1 + r_2)(1 + r_3)$$
$$= (1.20)(1.15)(1.10) = 1.518$$
$$Ln(1 + R_3) = \frac{Ln\ 1.1518}{3} = .139131$$
$$1 + R_3 = 1.1493$$
$$R_3 = .1493$$

An investment earning .1493 for three periods will be worth the same as an investment earning .20, .15, and .10. For example, we have for a $100 investment maturing at time 3:

$$100(1.1493)^3 = \$152$$
$$100(1.20)(1.15)(1.10) = \$152$$

We can use the yields to maturity to derive the forward rates. For example if we have R_3 and R_2:

$$1 + r_3 = \frac{(1 + R_3)^3}{(1 + R_2)^2} = \frac{(1.1493)^3}{(.1747)^2} = 1.10$$
$$r_3 = .10$$

If instead of single payment securities we have conventional bonds paying interest periodically and principal at maturity, the computation of the forward rates from the yields is more complex, but the same basic method of derivation is used.

Term Structure and Capital Budgeting

Assume an investment with the following cash flows:

Time	Cash Flows
0	−10,000
1	6,000
2	5,000
3	4,000

Using a constant interest rate of .20 (this is the current yield rate), we obtain:

Time	Cash Flows	Present Value Factors	PV
0	−10,000	$(1.20)^{-0}$	−10,000
1	6,000	$(1.20)^{-1}$	5,000
2	5,000	$(1.20)^{-2}$	4,167
3	2,090	$(1.20)^{-3}$	1,209
			NPV − 376

Using the same term structure as above where the present value of a dollar received at time n is:

$$PV = (1 + r_1)^{-1} (1 + r_2)^{-1} \ldots (1 + r_n)^{-1}$$

and

$$r_1 = .20, \; r_2 = .15, \; r_3 = .10$$

we obtain:

TIME	PV FACTORS	CASH FLOWS	PV
0	1.0000	−10,000	−10,000
1	.8333	6,000	5,000
2	.7246	5,000	3,623
3	.6588	2,090	1,377
			NPV 0

If the investment is undertaken the firm just breaks even: We start owing $10,000:

10,000	
+ 2,000	.20 interest
12,000	
− 6,000	payment of period 1
6,000	
+ 900	.15 interest
6,900	
− 5,000	payment of period 2
1,900	
190	.10 interest
2,090	
− 2,090	payment of period 3

Mutually Exclusive Investments

Consider two mutually exclusive investments. X has an internal rate of return of .18, and Y has an internal rate of return of .16.

While using the internal rate of return X seems to be more desirable, computing the net present values using the same term structure as above we find that Y is more desirable.

	0	1	2	3	IRR
X	−1,000	1,180			.18
Y	−1,000			+1,561	.16

NPV of X = $-1,000 + 1,180 (1.20)^{-1} = -1,000 + 983 = -17$
NPV of Y = $-1,000 + 1,561 (.6588) = -1,000 + 1,028 = 28$

Balloon Payment Debt

For every term structure (series of forward rates) there is an interest rate which when applied to a conventional balloon payment debt will leave the buyer of the debt indifferent. For example, assume a debt instrument with the following cash flows:

0	+ 1,000		
1	− 153.94 × .8333 =		128.18
2	− 153.94 × .7246 =		111.54
3	−1,153.94 × .6588 =		760.22
			1,000.04

This is equivalent in present value to the following variable interest debt:

0	+ 1,000
1	− 200
2	− 150
3	−1,100

	Conventional Debt, *$153.94 Interest*	*Variable Interest Debt,* *$200, $150, $100 Interest*
Owe	1,000	1,000
	× 1.20	× 1.20
	1,200	1,200

(*continued*)

	Conventional Debt, *$153.94 Interest*	*Variable Interest Debt,* *$200, $150, $100 Interest*	
Pay	153.94	200	interest
	1,046.06	1,000	
	× 1.15	×1.15	
	1,202.97	1,150	
Pay	153.94	150	interest
	1,049.03	1,000	
	× 1.10	×1.10	
	1,153.93	1,100	
Pay	1,153.93	1,100	interest and principal
	0	0	

We can say that debt paying .20, .15, .10 in sequence is equivalent to debt paying .1539 over the three years (with a balloon payment at maturity).

We shall now be able to decide by inspection which of the following two investments is acceptable:

	0	1	2	3	IRR
A	−1,000	153.94	153.94	1,153.94	.1539
B	−1,000	+1,160			.16

B yields .16, but the value or r_1 is .20; thus a .20 return is necessary for a one-period investment to be acceptable. Investment A will just break even (see the above calculations).

Comparing Present Value Factors

Table 10–1 shows the present value factors for a term structure of interest rates where the one period rates of successive periods are decreasing by .01. These present value factors are then compared to the present value factors obtained using .20 for each period. We see that the use of .20 for each period creates an artificially high obstacle for accepting investments, if we really believe that the normal forward rate is .11 and that the interest rates will gradually move to that value.

TABLE 10–1.   Different Interest Rates

Year	COL. 1 Interest Rate	COL. 2 Time Value Factor	COL. 3 Time Value Factors Using .20	COL. 4 = $\frac{\text{COL. 2}}{\text{COL. 3}}$ Ratio
1	.20	.8333	.8333	1.00
2	.19	.7003	.6944	1.01
3	.18	.5935	.5787	1.03
4	.17	.5072	.4823	1.05
5	.16	.4373	.4019	1.09
6	.15	.3802	.3349	1.14
7	.14	.3335	.2791	1.19
8	.13	.2952	.2326	1.27
9	.12	.2635	.1938	1.36
10	.11	.2374	.1615	1.47

Conclusions

Assume we read in a newspaper that a firm can borrow funds for one period at an interest rate of .20. It would be incorrect to use that rate to discount cash flows to be earned three periods from now unless one is willing to assume that the estimated one period rates of the next three periods are all equal to .20 and thus the three-period forward rate is .20.

The term structure concept introduces flexibility into the present value calculation and removes the requirement that the present value of a $1 at time n must be computed using $(1 + r)^{-n}$. Instead of one interest rate we can compute the present value using n different interest rates.

Key Ideas to Remember

1. Inflation tends to be accompanied by high interest rates.

2. There can be different interest rates for different periods. Using one average rate for several time periods can be misleading.

3. When short- and long-term rates diverge greatly, capital budgeting decisions should be made using a term structure of interest rates.

4. If one-period money costs .20 now, this does not mean .20 should be used to evaluate investments with long lives.

5. If the term structure is important, to compute a present value of a dollar at time n we should use

$$(1 + r_1)^{-1} (1 + r_2)^{-1} \ldots (1 + r_n)^{-1}$$

instead of $(1 + r)^{-n}$.

6. Debt of different maturities (durations) will have different costs, but we do not know which is cheapest unless we consider the borrowing rates at each maturity date (or more exactly the debt at each lending and borrowing date).

ELEVEN

Inflation and the Regulated Firm

In a regulated company
There's price control we learn,
Hence the value of an asset
Is the cash flow it can earn.

So if you are investing
While times are so inflated,
Give support to Ronald Reagan,
Or avoid what's regulated.

FMK

One objective of regulation is to allow a public utility to earn a fair return. This has been interpreted to mean a "comparable return" or a "capital attracting rate." The determination of the fair return is not an easy task.

There are two basic problems in determining the fair return. One is the determination of the rate base, and the second is the determination of the return to be allowed on the rate base. The determination of both of these factors is complicated by the presence of inflation.

It is important to realize that the basis of calculation will directly affect the nature of the common stock of a public utility.

Let us first assume a situation where both interest rates and prices are unchanging. The common stock of a public utility is then similar to a risky perpetual bond. For example, if the cost of stock equity is .10 and the amount of stock equity is $1,000,000, the firm will be allowed to earn $100,000 each year. If the firm is not successful in its efforts, then the stockholders will earn less than .10. The dividends are reduced or eliminated before the interest payments to debt holders are interrupted, but barring adverse circumstances the common stock is more like debt than an investment vehicle leading to the possibility of large gains.

Now we will relax one assumption and allow interest rates to change. This implies that the cost of equity will also change. While the cost of equity could be established at the time the capital is raised, this is not the conventional practice. The cost of equity capital is determined periodically and is likely to be considered to have changed if the interest rates have changed.

With changing interest rates (and changing costs of stock equity) the common stock of a regulated firm is similar to a variable interest rate debt. The investor in such a security will be facing an irregular dividend stream if dividends are a constant percentage of earnings. More likely, the level of earnings and the payout percentage will change but the board of directors will make an effort to have constant or systematically increasing dividends. Nevertheless, the earnings allowed to be earned by the firm on behalf of the stockholders will follow an irregular pattern as the interest rates change and the cost of equity capital is computed.

It is generally assumed that the cost of equity is a percentage return that applies to many time periods. In actual fact the cost of equity is more apt to be made up of a series of one-period spot rates, all different, ex ante as well as being different ex post.

Consider a situation where long term interest rates are .06 and it is agreed that the cost of equity is .10. If long term interest rates then increase from .06 to .14 it would be difficult to argue that the cost of stock equity did not also increase. If the increase in the cost of stock equity is allowed by the regulatory commission then we have the likelihood that the allowed return will fluctuate from period to period (where the period is defined to be the review cycle of the regulatory commission).

We will define the investors' total return as the cash dividends (likely to be constant or increasing) plus a capital gains component linked to the stockholders' total income. This total return will vary from period to period as the interest rate changes, as the allowed return changes, and as the actual income of the firm changes. Thus the investor may receive constant or increasing dividends but still have a fluctuating total return (the total return will be based on the market value of the common stock).

Price Level Adjustments to the Rate Base

We will now allow the price level to increase. One possibility is for the regulatory commission to ignore the price level adjusted rate base and use unadjusted cost.

While in the past the rate base had a "fair value" input, presently most regulatory commissions accept the cost based accounting measures of the firm as representing a reasonable basis for establishing an allowable return. This means that the common stock of a regulated firm is like a variable interest rate perpetual debt with a high degree of subordination and no legal penalty for a decreased dividend. It is not equivalent to the common stock of a firm operating in the normal competitive environment.

Assume the rate base of a firm stays constant at $100,000,000 using historical cost but the cost of equity starts at .10 and increases by .01 each year for five years. The allowed returns will be:

YEAR	ALLOWED RETURNS	ALLOWED INCOMES
1	.10	10,000,000
2	.11	11,000,000
3	.12	12,000,000
4	.13	13,000,000
5	.14	14,000,000

Now assume that it is decided to adjust the rate base for price level changes. There are many ways of accomplishing the adjustment. Assume the inflation rate is .12 per year. One possibility is to increase the adjusted rate base by .12 per year and allow the market return on the adjusted base. A second possibility is to allow the return that would be allowed if there were no inflation (say .10), on the price level adjusted rate base.
The results of both alternatives are:

YEAR	PRICE LEVEL ADJUSTED INVESTMENT	ALLOWED RETURN USING .10		ALLOWED RETURN USING THE MARKET RETURN
1	100,000,000	10,000,000	.10	10,000,000
2	112,000,000	11,200,000	.11	12,300,000
3	125,000,000	12,500,000	.12	15,000,000
4	140,000,000	14,000,000	.13	18,200,000
5	154,000,000	15,700,000	.14	21,980,000

It is logical that during an inflationary period with increasing interest rates the investors in the common stock of a public utility would prefer a price level adjusted rate base plus the use of the current market costs of stock equity capital. A common stock security for such a firm would maintain the real value of the investor's capital by allowing the current market return on the price level adjusted value of the investment. With .12 inflation, if we ignore the capital losses, to maintain real purchasing power of the income the investor would need:

YEAR	RETURN NEEDED TO MAINTAIN REAL PURCHASING POWER
1	10,000,000
2	11,200,000
3	12,500,000
4	14,000,000
5	15,700,000

Since the returns of the example (with price level adjusted rate base and increasing current cost of stock equity) more than maintain the real purchasing power of the income stream, we can expect this common stock to sell at a premium compared to the stock of a utility now allowed to adjust for inflation.

If the commission uses the price level adjusted rate base and the .10 allowed return (which does not include an inflation factor), then the allowed return will be exactly equal to the return needed to maintain the real purchasing power of the income stream. This would be an attractive security but would not necessarily sell at a premium. Note that it is reasonable to adjust the rate base, but if that is done, it is not appropriate that the current stock equity cost (reflecting inflation) be used, if the objective is to maintain the real value of the cash flow stream.

The Presence of Debt

Assume that in the above example the asset is 100% financed with debt paying .10 interest. The firm needs to be allowed to earn $10,000,000 per year, and there is no need to adjust the rate base for price level changes in order to give the debt holders the contractual amount of interest.

Thus the existence of debt complicates the analysis, since only the portion of the rate base financed by common stock (or the equivalent) must be adjusted for price level changes if any adjustment is to be made.

If the amount of debt is not taken into consideration, the common stockholders will reap a gain from the firm having used debt. The interest cost of the debt will be allowed. It is not necessary then to adjust the debt financed rate base for price level changes.

Depreciation Adjustment

Assume an asset with a one-year life costs $1,000 and is to be allowed to earn a .10 return. The income for the period will be $100, and the cash flow at time 1 will be $1,100.

Now if .12 inflation occurs, we know that the income at time 1 must be $112 in order to have $100 of purchasing power. But in addition the $1,000 of initial capital must be recovered. This means that $1,120 of capital must be recovered at time 1.
In total, the cash flows must be 1,120 + 112 = $1,232 at time 1. The income statement would be:

Revenues	$1,232
Price level adjusted depreciation	1,120
Income	$ 112

Thus we adjust both the rate base to $1,120 and the depreciation expense that will be deducted from the revenues in computing the income. The allowed return in this example is the same .10 as would be allowed with no inflation.

We obtain exactly the same result using the relation:

$$k = r + j + rj$$

where:

k is the inflation adjusted return
r is the allowed return with no inflation
j is the rate of inflation

The unadjusted cost of the investment and unadjusted depreciation expense will be used. We have now:

$$k = .10 + .12 + (.10)(.12) = .232$$

Now the income is .232 of $1,000, or $232. The income statement will be:

Revenues	$1,232
Depreciation	1,000
Income	$ 232

The cash flows of $1,232 are the same under both interpretations. The reported incomes would be different, since the depreciation expense is different with the two calculations.

In both cases the $1,232 of cash flows adjusted for inflation is $1,232/1.12 = $1,100, and thus a .10 real return on the initial investment of $1,000.

Again, if debt capital is being used where the debt receives a fixed interest rate, there is no need to adjust the depreciation expense of the asset (or the portion of the asset) financed with debt.

Price Level Adjustments and Regulation

Let us consider a situation where price level adjustments are not considered to be relevant by the regulatory commission. The commission uses the conventional cost based accounting measures to set rates and determine a fair return.

Assume the utility has a $1,000 fixed asset with an infinite life and the commission allows a .10 return. The firm will be allowed to earn $100 per year on this asset. If the market has a .10 time value factor, the present value of the earning (dividend) stream is $1,000.

Now assume that price level adjustment techniques are applied to the asset after a .20 inflation so that the asset is now recorded at $1,200. But the regulatory commission is still using cost and thus allow earnings of $100 a year. The market will value these earnings at $1,000. The $1,200 asset value and the resulting new value of stock equity will be misleading information to an investor in the common stock. Adjusting the plant assets for the inflation that has taken place is misleading. Given the policy of the regulatory authority, the asset, while having the physical characteristics of a real asset, has the economic characteristics of a monetary asset. It should not be adjusted as if it were real.

The conventional price level adjustments might be of intellectual interest, but they are not relevant to an investor unless the regulatory commission is going to use them to set the allowed return.

Conclusions

There are many ways that a public utility can be regulated in an inflationary environment. It is possible to mix and match so that the investors receive a bonanza, but price level adjustments per se are not such a bonanza.

It is possible that the adjustment of the rate base and depreciation expense for price level changes will actually reduce the overall cost of raising capital by eliminating one risk faced by investors, the risk of inflation. Given a history of high levels of inflation, it is possible that the adherence to historical cost by regulatory commissions might increase the cost of equity capital above what it would be if the investors were promised a return based on a price level adjusted rate base and price level adjusted depreciation expense.

Appendix I to this chapter is an extract from the 1980 annual report of Peoples Energy Corporation. Of particular interest is the explanation of the application of FAS 33 to the financial affairs of a regulated firm.

Key Ideas to Remember

1. The cost of equity of a public utility is determined for each specific year rather than at the time the capital is obtained. The cost of debt is defined at the time the capital is obtained.

2. If interest rates of debt change, we can expect that the cost of stock equity has also changed.

3. During inflation, common stock investors would prefer the use of a price level adjusted rate base and current market costs of stock equity capital.

4. The existence of fixed income debt affects the amount of the rate base that has to be adjusted to give the stockholders a fair return.

5. If price level adjustments are not recognized by the regulatory commission, use of the adjustments for accounting can be misleading.

6. For the value of a public utility's assets to change, the price setting authority must allow higher returns.

Appendix I: Peoples Energy Corporation's 1980 Annual Report

The Effect of Changing Prices (Unaudited)

The consolidated financial statements presented in this Annual Report reflect the historical cost of company assets. In accordance with the requirements of Financial Accounting Standards Board (FASB) Statement No. 33, entitled "Financial Reporting and Changing Prices," the two tables below provide an estimate of the effect of inflation on the company by presenting selected information on the basis of both conventional historical cost and constant dollars. Constant dollar amounts represent the restatement of historical costs in terms of dollars of equal purchasing power, as measured by the Consumer Price Index for All Urban Consumers.

The tables should be viewed as an estimate of the approximate effect of inflation rather than as a precise measure. Selected information on the basis of current costs will be provided in the Annual Report to the SEC on Form 10-K, also in accordance with Statement No. 33 requirements.

Under established practices, regulated companies are generally limited to the recovery of the historical cost of their properties in the rates charged to customers. When actual replacement of productive capacity is made by the regulated companies and the related depreciation expense is incurred, that company can file for both recovery of the increased depreciation expense and a return on the higher cost of replacement property. The amount by which the results of operations is affected is dependent, in part, upon the timeliness and extent of such rate increases and cannot be projected. During periods of inflation, the amounts recovered from customers will have less purchasing power than the historical dollars invested. As a result, the excess of the costs of regulated properties, stated in constant dollars, over historical cost is reflected as a reduction to net recoverable cost. Part of the loss in purchasing power from amounts invested in utility assets is offset from the use of long-term debt and other fixed return securities to finance a significant portion of these assets. These securities will be repaid with dollars that have less value than the dollars received when those securities were issued.

Depreciation expense included in the first table was developed by

Condensed Statement of Consolidated Income
Adjusted for Changing Prices

	HISTORICAL DOLLARS	CONSTANT DOLLAR*
	(millions)	
Operating revenues	$3,016	$3,016
Other income, net	42	42
	3,058	3,058
Costs and operating expenses	2,517	2,517
Depreciation, depletion and amortization)	168	312
Income deductions	118	118
Taxes on income	117	117
	2,920	3,064
Net income (excluding reduction to net recoverable cost)	$ 138	$ (6)
Reduction to net recoverable cost for regulated property		$ (54)
Reduction in purchasing power of net amounts owed		$ 125
Net		$ 71

* Average 1980 dollars

applying historical depreciation rates to the various property accounts after the accounts were adjusted for inflation. Storage gas inventories and gas costs were not repriced because purchased gas costs are recovered dollar-for-dollar through the rate-making process. In accordance with FASB guidelines, income taxes have not been adjusted.

TWELVE

Coping with Inflation

If you earn a fixed income,
Then indeed your future's glum!
Throw in the towel! Abandon hope!
There seems to be no way to cope.
                                    FMK

Inflation is not a special problem to all corporations. It is an opportunity for increased profits for some corporations and for some people, but it is a problem to a retired person on a fixed income, and to those corporations whose costs are increasing more rapidly than revenues.

It is well understood that many managers reject the first sentence of this chapter. In recent years corporations in non-OPEC countries have found it difficult to keep up with inflation. There is a tendency to equate inflation and the increase in energy costs.

Inflation means that the revenues and expenses of a firm will increase through time. If expenses (say, the cost of energy) increase more than revenues, the firm is harmed by changing prices. If the energy expense increase is caused by actions of government or foreign entities, then collectively corporations in a given country not gaining oil revenues are harmed by the inflation caused by the energy cost increase. Assume the actions of a monopolistic party (e.g., OPEC) cause the price increase in a factor of production, and the recovery of the expense increase is prevented by

151

competitive pressures. This set of circumstances will be harmful to profits.

Managers should be upset about monopolies which control products for which demand is inelastic, and should be disappointed that their products do not have the same inelastic demand characteristics so that the increased expenses can be recovered. It is not inflation per se that harms profits, but rather the lack of ability to increase prices sufficiently so that profits are maintained or increased.

A retired person on fixed income has no price increase decisions, and can only be harmed by inflation. The normal corporation at least has the possibility of controlling expenses and changing prices on the products it sells. While some corporations will be harmed by increases in all prices, other corporations will actually be benefited. For example, a corporation which has just completed a new hotel financed heavily with debt might welcome a shot of surprise inflation, since a large percentage of its costs (debt payments) are fixed by contract. On the other hand, a corporation which has entered into a contract to supply a given amount of a product for 10 years at a fixed price would find a surprise inflation to be a major disaster unless it has hedged its position by also contracting for its supplies on a fixed price basis.

Inflation and Maintenance of Real Income

We want to consider the effect of inflation on income, given the presence of income taxes. We will consider the effect on wages and interest income.

A Wage Earner

Assume a wage of $40,000, an inflation rate of 10%, and a tax rate of .4. What does a wage earner need in the way of wage increase to maintain real income?

The answer is not surprising. With 10% inflation the worker needs a 10% wage increase. The after tax income is $24,000 with $40,000 of pretax income. After the 10% inflation the after tax income has to be $26,400 to maintain real income of $24,000. If we add 10% to $40,000 we obtain $44,000. The after tax income is $44,000 $(1-.4)$ = $26,400.

Thus the before tax income only has to increase at the same rate as the inflation rate to maintain the real income of the wage earner. If the average tax rate were to increase with the increase in income, the amount of the required increase would change.

If the new averge tax rate is .55 rather than .40, we would need $58,667 of before tax income. The tax would be $32,267, and the wage earner would net $26,400, which has purchasing power of $24,000 in beginning of the period purchasing power.

Now we will consider the same type of problem from the point of view of an investor in debt type of securities.

One-Shot Inflation: Debt

If there is a *one shot* price change and the desire is to maintain the purchasing power of interest flows (not the principal), then the interest rate must be increased by the same percentage as the price change. If prices were to increase 10%, the interest payments would have to increase 10% to maintain the purchasing power of the investor.

For example, if perpetual bonds were paying .04 with zero inflation and .024 after tax (the personal tax rate is .4), then with a 10% one-shot inflation the investor would require a .044 interest rate, which is $.044 (1 - .4) = .0264$ after tax. This is 10% higher than .024 and leads to a maintenance of purchasing power of the after tax interest at the new plateau of prices.

With zero inflation an investor with a $1,000 bond would earn $40 before tax and $24 after tax.

With 10% one-shot inflation the investor earning $44 would have $26.40 after tax and $26.40/1.10 = 24$ real dollars, so the purchasing power of the cash flow is maintained. The purchasing power of the principal has not been maintained.

Repetitive Inflation

Now we will assume an annual rate of inflation of j.

We have a multiperiod security and are maintaining the purchasing power of the interest and principal. We have for the before tax return required to maintain the investor's purchasing power:

$$k = r + j + rj$$

where j is the annual rate of inflation and the r is the real return.

If we have a personal tax rate of t_p, then with zero inflation the investor earning a real return of r earns after tax:

$$i = (1 - t_p)r$$

With inflation we want:

$$(1 - t_p)k = i + j + ij$$

so that the after tax real return is still:

$$i = (1 - t_p)r$$

Example

Assume $t_p = .4$ and $r = .05$; then the investor earns after tax:

$$i = (1 - t_p)r = (1 - .4).05 = .03$$

With .20 inflation we have:

$$(1 - t_p)k = i + j + ij$$
$$.6k = .03 + .20 + .006$$
$$k = .393$$

With a $1,000 investment paying .05 and no inflation, the investor nets $30 of interest after tax and $1,030 in total.

With .20 inflation and a debt paying .393, the investor has $393 of income plus the principal or $1,393 before tax. The tax is .40 of $393 or $157 so the investor nets $1,236 after tax. The $1,236 divided by 1.20 to deflate for price level change is $1,030 real which is the same net as was obtained when there was no inflation and the debt paid .05.

The example illustrates the difficulty of keeping up with inflation using fixed income securities when nominal interest is taxed with no consideration given to the maintenance of real income.

The example used a .40 tax rate. A larger tax rate would make the results even more dramatic. But even with a .4 tax rate and .20 inflation we needed an interest rate of .393 in order to give the same real return as a .05 debt with no inflation.

The wage earner example showed the difficulty of maintaining real income if the average tax rate increases with the dollar (not the purchasing power) income.

The interest example shows the difficulty of maintaining real wealth using a fixed income security in the presence of the present tax laws. Investors are apt to shift to investments that are taxed differently than bonds (or debt in general) if they desire to maintain their real wealth.

Inflation and Operations

When does a firm benefit from inflation?

We will suggest a simple type of test. Consider a person on a fixed income of $20,000 per year with zero assets and liabilities. Now give that person the choice between constant prices and a .20 annual inflation. It is not difficult to conclude how a rational person will choose. The income does not change with inflation, but the cost of living will increase. The person will opt for constant prices.

In the above situation the analysis was simplified by the assumption that there were no assets and no liabilities. The same conclusion could also have been reached if there were monetary assets exactly equal to the liabilities, or if there were real assets financed completely by the owners (no debt). This assumes the price index correctly measures the change in value of the real assets.

Now let us consider a corporation with revenues and expenses, and initially we shall assume the monetary asset–liability positions balance out.

In determining whether or not such a corporation is harmed by inflation, we have to know how the revenues and the expenses will be affected by the price changes.

If both the revenues and expenses changed by the same percentage as the price level changed, the firm is not harmed by inflation. It holds its own. Example:

The firm is currently earning $2,000 per year:

Revenues	$10,000
Expenses	8,000
Income	$ 2,000

With inflation of .20 we assume the revenues and expenses will both increase by .20:

	Current Period	Next Period with .20 Inflation
Revenue	$10,000	$12,000
Expenses	8,000	9,600
Income	$ 2,000	$ 2,400

Income increases by .20, which is just sufficient to maintain the current period's income in real terms.

If we inject the fact that some of the expenses do not change with inflation (e.g., depreciaiton), then the possibility of a firm breaking even with inflation is enhanced. It is further enhanced if the total liabilities (fixed dollar claims) exceed the monetary assets. The financing of real assets with debt is a way of increasing the possibility of profiting from inflation if the cost of the debt does not perfectly reflect the expected inflation.

If revenues and expenses are affected differently by inflation, then the safest procedure is to compute the effect of the inflation. For example, in the above situation assume revenues increase by .20 and expenses by .10 when there is a .20 inflation. We then have the firm benefiting from the inflation:

	Current Period	*Next Period with .20 Inflation*
Revenue	$10,000	$12,000
Expenses	8,000	8,800
Income	$ 2,000	$ 3,200

If we had assumed that revenues increased by .10 and expenses by .20, the firm would have been harmed by the .20 inflation. To predict the effect of inflation on a firm, we need to know the elasticities of revenue and expenses with respect to changes in prices measured by the price index.

Net Real Assets

We will now assume the firm's real assets are partially financed with debt, so that the firm will have a monetary gain from inflation (a more exact statement of the assumption is that liabilities exceed the monetary assets).

Assume that there is a .20 inflation but both revenues and expenses only increase by .10, so that a comparison of revenues and expenses indicates the firm is worse off in real income terms:

	Current Period	*Next Period with .20 Inflation*
Revenues	$10,000	$11,000 (10% increase)
Expenses	8,000	8,800
Income	$ 2,000	$ 2,200

But now assume the following balance sheets apply:

CONVENTIONAL ACCOUNTING

	Beginning of Next Period	End of Next Period
Real assets	50,000	52,200
Debt	40,000	40,000
Stock equity	10,000	12,200

We will assume the $8,800 includes the interest cost on the $40,000 debt. Also, for simplicity we assume the revenues and expenses all take place at year end (this is consistent with FAS 33).

In terms of year end dollars the beginning debt was $48,000 and there was a $8,000 monetary gain from being in debt. Instead of a $2,200 income, the total income in year end dollars is $10,200. In year end dollars the two balance sheets are:

CONSTANT DOLLARS

	Beginning of Next Period	End of Next Period
Real assets and other	60,000	62,200
Debt	48,000	40,000
Stock equity	12,000	22,200

At the beginning of the next period the stockholders had command over $12,000 of resources in terms of year end dollars. At the end of the next period the stockholders had command over $22,200 of resources. This is an improvement for the year of $10,200.

Note that before considering the relative well-being of the firm at two moments in time, we have to consider the monetary gains and losses. Since monetary gains and losses do not affect the earnings per share following FAS 33, the interpretation of information resulting from the application of FAS 33 requires expert interpretation.

Before concluding whether or not a firm is harmed or helped by inflation, a complete pro forma constant dollar accounting analysis would have to be done, and these results would have to be compared to the results with zero inflation.

The appendix to this chapter presents a model for determining whether a firm is benefited by inflation.

Accounting Measures

The manager who is aware of the limitations of accounting under inflationary conditions is fortunate. At least there is awareness of the fact that the information has limitations. Without inflation, the manager might be lulled into accepting the accounting measures as being perfectly correct. Consider the attempt to measure managerial performance. There are many difficulties to using accounting information. Inflation highlights the necessity of using judgment.

Financial Decisions

The threat of inflation will tend to increase the cost of both debt and common stock capital. If the debt holders (and prospective purchasers of debt) anticipate inflation, there is no reason to expect one type of capital to have a lower cost than other types of capital because of the inflation. Other institutional factors (such as the tax laws) might well affect the preference.

The decision rule to accept or reject investments is theoretically simple. If the net present value is positive, the investment is acceptable. However, determining the cash flows and adjusting for time value and risk are not that simple.

One useful generalization is that if the rate of inflation is larger than the borrowing rate, investing in real assets is likely to be a desirable strategy. The necessary assumption is that the real assets will increase in value at the same rate as the inflation so the return will exceed the cost of borrowing the funds to finance the investment. Unfortunately, inflation rates are averages, and some prices will increase in value more than the inflation rate and some will increase less. It takes more than a positive inflation rate to insure that an investment in a real asset financed by debt will be desirable.

Are Profits Adequate?

The above question is frequently asked. Is the level of current profits adequate to supply the capital necessary to replace or expand the current stock of capital?

We will first consider an investment chain with no inflation and then add inflation.

Assume the time value factor is .10 and a firm has an asset which cost $2,487 and promises to return $1,000 a year for three years. We will assume further that investors are paid .10 each year on the decreasing investment plus a .10 return on the remaining cash flows that are set aside for an asset replacement fund. This translates to the investors being paid $248.70 each year on a constant total investment of $2,487:

PERIOD	CASH FLOW	PAYMENT TO INVESTORS	RESIDUAL	RESIDUAL PLUS .10 INTEREST PER YEAR ON FUND
1	1,000	248.70	751.30	909
2	1,000	248.70	751.30	826
3	1,000	248.70	751.30	751
				2,486

Now the firm has $2,486 at the end of three years and the investor has received a .10 return on the capital invested.

With no change in the price level, at the end of three years the firm can buy another edition of the asset costing $2,487 and repeat the cycle. Capital is being maintained.

If the asset had been financed with debt costing .10, the entire $1,000 of cash flow would have been used to pay the interest and principal of the debt. At time 3 the firm would have zero capital and zero debt. The stockholders would break even.

Even with common stock it is more likely that the funds will be returned to investors or will be invested in other long-lived assets than that they will be set aside in an asset replacement fund. Nevertheless, the above example is consistent with a conclusion that funds can be set aside to replace the asset at the end of its life. The funds so set aside are adequate for replacement.

Now let us assume inflaton of .12 per year, so that the $2,487 asset will cost $2,487(1.12)^3 = $3,494$ at the end of three years. In addition we will inflate the cash flows of each year:

Period	Unadjusted Cash Flow	Price Level Adjustment	Nominal Dollars
1	1,000	1.12	1,120
2	1,000	1.12^2	1,254
3	1,000	1.12^3	1,405

Assume the payment to the current investors is fixed. The capital is in the form of debt costing .10. In the previous example (zero inflation) the firm ends up at time 3 with zero capital. Now the residual after debt payments of $1,000 per year will be:

Period	Residual	Residual Plus .10 Interest Per Year
1	120	145
2	254	279
3	405	405
	Total	829

At the end of three years the firm will have $829 toward the purchase of the more expensive asset (which will now cost $3,494). Previously it had zero dollars at the end of three years toward the purchase of an asset that cost $2,487. We could change the rate of inflation compared to the cost of money and rate at which the funds can be reinvested and obtian different numbers for the amount of capital the firm has.

Now let us assume that the capital used was common stock and that the firm pays $248.70 each period to the investors. At the end of three periods, with a .10 interest rate and .12 inflation, the firm will have $3,316:

Period	Cash Flow	Capital Payment	Residual	Residual plus .10 Interest	Residual Plus .16 Interest
1	1,120	248.70	871.30	1,054	1,172
2	1,254	248.70	1,005.30	1,106	1,166
3	1,405	248.70	1,156.30	1,156	1,156
				3,316	3,494

The asset costs $3,494, whereas with a .10 reinvestment rate the firm has only accumulated $3,316. If the reinvestment rate had increased to .16 reflecting inflationary expectations, the firm would have $3,494, which is just sufficient to buy the new asset.

In the above example we allowed the cash flows of the asset to increase consistent with inflation, we paid the old capital contributors an amount that was not adjusted for inflation, and in addition we increased the rate that reinvested funds can earn to .16. With these reasonable assumptions we end up with enough capital to finance the new edition of the asset costing an inflated $3,494.

Now let us assume that the cash flows of the asset do not change but rather remain at $1,000 per period, so that at the end of three years the firm has a worn-out asset, $2,487 cash, and an indication that a new edition of the asset would cost $3,494.

Remember that the cash flows are unchanged, so that the asset promises to pay $1,000 per year for three years. If this investment is discretionary, it will be rejected. The asset returns $3,000 in total over its useful life and costs $3,494. The investment is not acceptable with any nonnegative interest rate. Until the economic conditions improve for this firm (or industry), productive assets should not be replaced. The $2,487 cash that is held should be invested elsewhere or should be returned to investors. The economic facts are saying that there is excess capacity and the current prices do not justify making the investment of $3,494.

As the capacity of the industry shrinks, all things equal, we can expect prices of this product to increase relative to other prices, and for the investment to again become desirable. But at the end of the first three-year cycle it is not desirable to invest $3,494 to earn $1,000 per year for three years.

The current profits relate to the past investment. They tell little about the firm's ability to replace the current stock of long-lived assets with a new generation.

The ability of the firm to replace the assets will depend on the dividend policy of the firm, whether the original assets were financed with debt, the level of profits in each year, the reinvestment rate, and the cost of replacing the assets. There is no easy general method of determining whether or not the level of profits is adequate to replace the assets currently being used.

Capital Availability

Top level managers are concerned about whether or not inflation will affect the availability of capital. We will consider the issue from two points of view.

First, we will discuss whether or not a capital shortage can actually exist for society. Second, we will consider the question from the point of view of a corporation trying to raise capital.

We live in a world of scarcity; thus in one sense there is always less capital than we would like. Individuals always want roads paved, bridges built, better parks, and nicer hotels. Corporate managers want more efficient machines and computers as well as more capacity. So at one level there always is a capital shortage.

At another level there is never a capital shortage. If the demand for capital shifts, the price (cost) of capital changes so that the equality of the suppply of and demand for capital is maintained.

Inflation can affect the willingness of people to save for the future and thus cause a shift in the supply curve for capital. This shift will cause the equilibrium cost of capital to be higher (and the amount of capital used to be decreased), so that there is less capital made available than some planners would desire. Basically the problem is the split between the amount of a country's gross production which is allocated toward consumption and the amount allocated toward investment. Inflation is one factor, but such factors as government regulation (e.g., control of prices and profits) are another, as is the tax policy dealing with investment at both the corporate and individual levels.

If an investor can earn .04 with zero inflation and can earn .1648 with a .12 inflation, there is no reason (with zero taxes) why the amount invested should differ because of the presence or absence of inflation. In both cases the investor is earning a .04 real return. If with the .12 inflation the investor can only earn .10 because of government action, the amount invested will likely decrease. Also, if the above numbers are all before personal taxes, the after tax measures are likely to be such that again investment will be discouraged. Thus inflation combined with government imposed factors can adversely affect the amount committed to investment.

If the amount of capital committed is decreased and if interest rates are artificially kept low, corporations raising capital will have to pay less in real terms for their capital than with zero inflation. Thus with .12 inflation a corporation may be able to borrow funds at .12. This is a zero real cost. However, if this situation were to continue for any length of time we would expect a corporation to be unable to obtain the amount of capital it wants at the given cost. Attempts by corporations to raise the capital they wish to invest will tend to fuel the inflation if government pumps in the money to keep interest rates low.

Given the nature of capital markets a corporation can always raise an amount of capital consistent with its size *if* it is willing to pay a large enough cost. There are three situations when a firm cannot (or will not) use debt:

1. The firm might be up against its debt capacity (the rate of interest necessary to attract the capital will force the firm into bankruptcy), or the firm is not willing to accept the risk added by the debt.
2. The cost of the debt is too high compared to the expected returns of the investments being considered.
3. The lenders will not lend to a firm of the given credit standing of the firm, given a capital shortage (created by artificially low interest rates).

Of course, if debt is not feasible, the firm can shift to the use of some form of equity. For example, common stock can be issued if the dilution necessary to achieve the issuance is not considered to be excessive, or more funds can be retained rather than paid as dividends.

When managers state that capital is not available because of inflation, they generally mean that capital is not available at a cost or price they would like. There is no essential reason why an increase in the general price level should necessarily lead to less capital being available than with zero inflation or why the capital being raised will have a higher real cost with inflation than with constant prices.

Alternative Securities

In an earlier example we found that in order to earn a .03 after tax real return, with a .4 tax rate and a .20 inflation, it was necessary to earn .393 per year interest. It is very difficult for an investor in conventional debt to stay even with inflation if taxes are considered. The investor is likely to seek out investments where increments in value are not taxed currently. These investments include collectibles (art, coins, stamps, etc.) and real estate.

Common stock is another possibility if the dividend policy of the firm is sensible.

There are some zero tax or low tax investors who will find straight debt attractive if the interest rate is sufficiently high (.26 will be adequate with a .20 inflation and a .05 real interest return desired). But an alternative strategy to attract investors not wanting to pay high nominal interest rates is to give some type of equity kicker.

The most common form of debt security with an equity kicker is a convertible bond. Detachable warrants with a relatively low exercise price are also a way of obtaining debt funds. A third type of arrangement is for the lender to share in the profits if they exceed a defined level or to make the debt convertible into equity. A fourth possibility is for the lender to buy both debt and common stock in the firm needing the capital. A fifth possibility is to have the debt convertible into a real asset, such as silver or gold, at the option of the holder.

All of the above alternatives have the effect of making the lender an equity participant in the financing or the holder of a real asset. Recognizing the difficulty of making a real after tax return from investing in straight debt, the investor shifts to a mixture of debt and common stock (in some form).

Flexible Yields

Inflation tends to be accompanied by increasing interest rates, which depress prices of outstanding long-term bonds. The threat of even higher interest rates makes the issuance of additional debt with a long maturity more difficult.

A solution to this problem has been to issue securities with flexible yields. The floating rates are computed periodically based on the rates of government securities (ranging from 13-week Treasury bills to 30-year Treasury bonds), but the yields of other securities could just as easily be used.

With floating rate securities the bondholder will not suffer a significant loss because of an increase in interest rates. One risk is eliminated.

An Alternative to Constant Dollar Accounting

Constant dollar accounting starts with the cost of an asset and applies a price index relative to convert to constant dollars. This method of accounting is cost based, since costs are being adjusted for changes in purchasing power.

An alternative to constant dollar accounting which incorporates a measure of the general price level inflation is to use value estimates for all assets. The difficulty with the procedure is that value estimates may be difficult to obtain and are likely to require a degree of subjectivity. The advantage of value measures is that year end value measures are likely to be more relevant for a decision maker than price level adjusted cost information, if one can rely on the estimates of value.

As a first step it would be useful if value measures were used in those situations where they are readily available. For example, value measures should be used to value all widely traded securities and all basic homogeneous commodities which have well-defined market prices.

Some Conclusions

With zero inflation the price of a product and the costs of making the product will still change. A positive inflation rate does not change the tasks to be done, but merely makes the forecasting more difficult since there is now a larger variance attached to the distribution of possible outcomes. Thus inflation makes the manager's job more interesting.

If a manager's total business experience has been to pay interest at the rate of between .05 and .10, it is not surprising that a rate of .15 is labeled as a high rate. But before .15 can be called high, it is necessary to consider the inflation rate. With a .20 inflation rate, .15 is a very low (a negative) real rate to pay for funds. Inflation requires that we shift from the sole use of money to measure events to the use of real purchasing power for evaluating changes through time. It will take time, but sooner or later the cost of capital will be defined in real terms rather than nominal terms when the adjectives "high" and "low" are applied.

Key Ideas to Remember

1. Inflation does not adversely affect all corporations.

2. A wage earner receiving the same percentage wage increase as the inflation rate would stay even with inflation except for the progressiveness of the income tax.

3. Taxes make it very difficult to earn a real return with fixed income debt if there is substantive inflation.

4. If debt holders anticipate inflation, debt might not be a bargain to an issuing corporation (especially if the investor is subject to taxation of income).

5. Inflation might cause common stock to be a more desirable form of capital than debt, if the debt holders are able to demand a real after tax return.

6. We can expect alternative securities having some of the characteristics of common stock to become more prevalent as investors subject to tax learn it is difficult to earn a positive real return with fixed income debt.

7. A sensible investment strategy during inflation is to invest in real assets. Real estate and common stock fit into this category. Success is not guaranteed, but at least it is possible. Debt must yield a significantly higher return than the inflation rate to be a good investment.

Appendix 1

We want to determine necessary conditions for a firm to benefit from inflation.

Let: j be the inflation rate

R be the net revenue (all revenues and out of pocket expenses move at the same rate)

t be the corporate tax rate

i be the price change of R

I be the interest expense

B be the debt principal payment

D be the depreciation expense

We will assume that the basic revenue is R and R only changes with i.

We will first assume zero debt. With no price change at time one, the firm nets

$$R(1 - t) + tD$$

With a price change of i and inflation of j the firm nets cash flows at time one of

$$(1 + i) R(1 - t) + tD.$$

The price level adjusted value of these cash flows is:

$$\frac{(1 + i) R(1 - t) + tD}{1 + j}$$

The price level adjusted value is larger than the value with no price changes if:

$$\frac{(1 + i) R(1 - t) + tD}{1 + j} > R(1 - t) + tD.$$

Simplifying

$$(i - j) R(1 - t) > j t D$$

and it is necessary that:

$$i > \frac{j t D + j R(1 - t)}{R(1 - t)} = \frac{j(tD + R(1 - t))}{R(1 - t)}$$

for the firm to benefit from inflation.

Let $R = 100$, $t = .40$, $D = 20$, $j = .10$, $tD = \$8$, $R(1 - t) = \$60$

$$i > \frac{.10 (8 + 60)}{60} = \frac{6.8}{60} = .113$$

With the above facts the firm benefits in real terms if its prices increase by .113 when all prices increase by .10.

We will now assume that debt is used to finance the asset so that with zero inflation:

$$R(1 - t) + tD - B - I + tI = 0$$

With inflation the cash flows are:

$$(1 + i) R(1 - t) + tD - B - I + tI$$

The price level adjusted value with inflation is:

$$\frac{(1 + i) R(1 - t) + tD - B - (1 - t)I}{1 + j}$$

Continuing the example let $B = 62.39$ and $I = \$9.36$. Then with zero inflation the firm just breaks even.

$$R(1-t) + tD - B - (1-t)I = 60 + 8 - 62.39 - (1-.4)\,9.36$$
$$= 5.61 - 5.61 = 0$$

With .10 inflation *and* a .10 increase in corporate prices we have

$$\frac{(1 + i) R(1 - t) + tD - B - (1 - t)I}{1 + j} = \frac{1.10 (60) + 8 - 62.39 - 5.61}{1.10}$$

$$= \frac{74 - 62.39 - 5.61}{1.10} = \frac{74 - 68}{1.10}$$

$$= \frac{6}{1.10} = \$5.45$$

The real value is increased by inflation now that the asset is financed with debt.

Conclusions

A firm may benefit from inflation even where its net revenues do not increase more rapidly than inflation. In fact, the corporation might benefit from inflation even if the firm's prices increase at a lower rate than inflation (the existence of debt is required as a necessary but not sufficient condition).

Index

Index